WITHDRAWN

Mallarmé
and
The Language of Mysticism

Mallarmé

and

The Language of Mysticism

Thomas A. Williams

The University of Georgia Press

For Christina
For Andrea and Lisa
And for my Son.

Quand les mythologies s'effondrent,
c'est dans la poésie que trouve
refuge le divin.

St.-Jean Perse

Contents

Preface

By way of preface, I would like to call the reader's attention to two facts about the general orientation of this work.

First, its intent is synthetic and not analytic. What is attempted is an organic interpretation of the whole of Mallarmé's work, specifically of that work as it appears in context of mystical experience and the modes of expression traditionally associated with it. Hopefully, such an interpretation will prove of value to those who undertake the explication of individual poems. But explication *per se* is not my purpose. I am not attending to the obscurities and difficulties of this particular poem or that one, but working toward the grand theme which ties them all together.

Second, a word of caution about words like "mystic" and "mysticism." I use them here in a broader sense than the one customarily understood in the context of western Christianity, and I trust the reader will follow me in this usage. Mystical consciousness is essentially timeless, and prior to any creed which may be imposed upon it.

Thomas Williams

Davidson, North Carolina
July 1969

Any final answer to the question of the nature of mysticism may be reserved uniquely for the mystics themselves since one of the most nearly universal characteristics of their experience, according to the widest range of historical and contemporary testimony, is that it is indescribable. One sees, one feels, one knows, but one cannot tell. Seemingly, no mystic has ever been completely satisfied with his efforts to communicate his own vision. What, then, is mysticism? Our own approach to the question will be to begin with what is perhaps obvious, and then go ahead slowly, letting the complexities of the problem unfold gradually before us.

The first condition of mystical insight is the presence of a deep spiritual sense of the mystery of being, of the isolation of consciousness surrounded by the void, of light by darkness, of multiplicity by unity, of time by eternity—a sense that, as William James said, "the further limits of our being plunge . . . into an altogether different dimension of existence from the merely 'understandable' world."[1] The potential mystic also possesses a sense of the division, of the fragmentation of some primeval, timeless Whole into the finite and mortal fragments which today make up man and man's world, and he longs for its reintegration. There was Eden, and then there was the Fall; and the Fall, as Coleridge pointed out, in its creation of self-consciousness, was the "creation of the non-absolute."[2] In Mallarmé, as we shall see, the vision of perfect oneness perhaps existed in the piety of his youth. Then followed the divisiveness, the breaking up of one term into two, as he felt himself separated from the Godhead. The azure, serene in its irony, became the implacable enemy of human consciousness. This schism led through a profound psychic disintegration to final revelation and reconciliation.

Logically, eternity and infinity are only symbols for the incomprehensible, which stands at the limits of all rational thought. They are words which denote the boundary beyond which even the most audacious systems of thought—to the degree that they are systems—cannot progress, the horizon of irrationality which surrounds all merely logical truth.

Alfred de Vigny said that "tout homme a vu le mur qui borne son esprit." Insofar as *esprit* means *mind*, as it does here, Vigny's observation is certainly true. No matter how far the mind ventures, the wall is always there. "Consciousness," Evelyn Underhill says, "is always running out to the encounter of the absolute and being forced to return."[3]

Now, for the mystic, very little matters except what lies *beyond* the confining wall. Time and space and the categories of reason become his chief enemies. "Nothing hinders the soul's knowledge of God," says Meister Eckhart, "as much as time and space, for time and space are fragments, whereas God is One." And therefore, he continues, "if the soul is to know God, it must know him above time and outside of space; for God is neither this nor that as are all manifested things."[4]

In these terms, the mystic is the person who possesses what J. H. Leuba, in his *The Psychology of Religious Mysticism*, calls the "will to union" so intensely that through some mysterious short-circuit of the mind he actually does manage to transcend the limiting categories and, in the space of a moment, achieve such intense and unutterable experience of and even identification with the absolute, or with God, or with whatever else he may choose to call it, that the experience literally makes him over into a new person.[5] Note that we said the Absolute *or* God. The nomenclature is not of the essence. In his *Mysticism and Philosophy,* W. T. Stace shows that even atheism is not incompatible with mysticism. No, the mystic is not identifiable through his creed, but through his mission, his "spiritual and intangible quest"[6] for the lost Eden, his search for the "pre-existent meaning hidden in the chaos of life."[7] But the mystic does not *think* his way through to his unitary paradise. Somehow the interior ground is prepared, and suddenly Eden is there. *Le coeur a ses raisons que la raison ne connaît point.*

Most often, insight comes during what can be characterized as a totally abnormal intensity of perception which may endure for no more than one or two brief and privileged moments. Stace quotes the words of one N. M., whom he identifies only as "an intellectual." N. M. describes an experience he had one day as he looked out of the window of a tenement in Brooklyn:

> Suddenly every object in my field of vision took on a curious and intense existence of its own; that is, everything appeared to have an 'inside'—to exist as I existed, having inwardness, a kind of individual life, and every object, seen under this aspect, appeared exceedingly beautiful. There was a cat out there, with its head lifted, effortlessly watching a wasp that moved without moving, just above its head. . . . Everything was urgent with life . . . which was the same in the cat, the wasp, the broken bottles, and merely manifested itself differently in these individuals. All things seemed to glow with a light that came from within them. I experienced complete certainty that at that moment I saw things as they really were, and I was filled with grief at the realization of the real situation of human beings, living continuously in the midst of all this without being aware of it. . . . I saw that all ugliness was a wounding of life. . . . I began to be aware of time again, and the impression of entering into time was as marked as though I had stepped from air to water, from a rarer to a thicker element.[8]

This experience is certainly personal enough, and is not related in any way to any system of organized thought, philosophical or theological. Its felt value is prior to anything thought might make of it. N. M., for some mysterious reason, has been afforded a spontaneous, atemporal vision of the unity of being, a vision which appears to him "exceedingly beautiful."

Here now is an experience which R. M. Bucke, a Canadian psychiatrist at the turn of the century, relates in his book on what he calls the "cosmic" consciousness.

> I had spent the evening in a great city, with two friends, reading and discussing poetry and philosophy. We parted at midnight. I had a long drive in a hansom to my lodging. My mind, deeply under the influence of the ideas, images, and emotions called up by the reading and the talk, was calm and peaceful. I was in a state of quiet, almost passive, enjoyment, not actually thinking, but letting ideas, images and emotions flow of themselves, as it were, through my head. All at once, without any warning of any kind, I found myself wrapped in a flame-colored cloud. For an instant I thought of fire, an immense conflagration somewhere close by in that great city; the next, I knew that the fire was within myself. Directly afterward there came upon me a sense of exultation, of immense joyousness accompanied or immediately followed by an intellectual illumination impossible to describe. Among other things, I did not merely come to believe, but I saw that the universe is not composed of dead matter, but is, on the contrary, a living Presence; I became conscious in myself of eternal life. It was not a conviction that I would have eternal life, but a consciousness that I possessed eternal life then; I saw that all men are immortal; that the cosmic order is such that without any peradventure all things work together for the good of each and all; that the foundation principle of the world, of all the worlds is what we call love, and that the happiness of each and all is in the long run absolutely certain. The vision lasted a few seconds and was gone; but the memory of it and the sense of reality of what it taught has remained during the quarter of a century which had elapsed since. I knew that what the vision showed was true. I had attained to a point of view from which I saw that it must be true. That view, that conviction, I may say, that consciousness has never, even during periods of the deepest depression, been lost.[9]

Reflecting on his own experience and on similar ones he had studied, Dr. Bucke concluded that "the prime characteristic of the cosmic consciousness is a consciousness of . . . the life and order of the universe. Along with the consciousness of the cosmos," he continued, "there occurs an intellectual enlightenment which alone would place the individual on a new plane of existence—would make him almost a member of a new species." The mental state accompanying the enlightenment, said Dr. Bucke, was one dominated by "an indescribable feeling of elevation, elation, and joyousness," and by a conviction that eternal life is not something reserved for a future time, but something in which one is actually participating.[10]

The essential elements are all present: absolute conviction of the truth of the revelation, a heightened power of perception which reveals fundamental unity and eternity of self and the world, and the subsequent transformation of the level of consciousness to that of a "new species."

Descriptions of similar experiences abound in the literature of the nineteenth and twentieth centuries as romantic thought advances from an early, rather naive infatuation with the self to an understanding of the possibilities and techniques of its metaphysical exploitation. This is the current which runs through Nerval and Baudelaire to Rimbaud and Mallarmé, and which, coming into our own century through Proust, Bergson, and the surrealists, gives much of its spiritual coloring to contemporary literature. Arthur Koestler, in jail in Spain, experiences a kind of dissolution into "the universal pool," a "universal expansion," an "oceanic feeling" which brings with it a "draining of all tensions, the absolute catharsis, the peace that passeth all understanding."[11] Hart Crane writes to his friend Gorhan Munson that "at times . . . I feel an enormous power within me that seems almost supernatural." His mind has "spiraled to a kind of seventh heaven of consciousness and egoistic dance among the spheres," and he has heard "something like an objective voice which kept saying . . . 'You have the higher consciousness. . . . This is something that very few have . . . !' " Afterwards, he relates, "a happiness, ecstatic such as I have known only twice in 'inspirations' came over me. I felt in two worlds. And at once . . . O Gorhan," he concludes, "I have known moments in eternity."[12]

Particularly valuable is Aldous Huxley's account in *The Doors of Perception* of a mescaline-induced state of "higher consciousness." Whether or not one feels that records of such artificially-induced mystic states should be considered a part of the literature of mysticism, one must admit that they furnish—especially when they take place under near laboratory conditions, as this one did—invaluable information on the psychic state of the mystic. It helps too that Huxley was already thoroughly familiar with the literature in the field.

Huxley agrees with the idea of Bergson that the main function of the human brain is eliminative, that it culls out of our perception all that is not necessary to, and indeed, all that might be harmful to, adaptation and survival. The brain is an eminently practical organ, a "reducing valve"[13] through which only that which is useful is normally allowed to pass.

The mystic state, says Huxley, whether natural or induced, effectively by-passes the reducing function of the mind. It projects its visions elsewhere than on the coordinates of time and space: "Place and distance cease to be of much interest. The mind does its perceiving in terms of intensity of existence, profundity of significance, relationships within a pattern. . . ." What is important is not "measures and location," but "being and meaning," and the "obscure knowledge that All is in all, that All is actually each." For Huxley, this is "as near . . . as a finite mind can come to 'perceiving everything that is happening everywhere in the universe.' "[14]

Shortly after swallowing his dose of mescaline, Huxley's glance falls on a vase which contains three flowers. Some moments before he had not even noticed them, but now they quiver with intense life and deep meaning. Their real existence, their living presence, it seems to Huxley, shows up Plato's realm of ideas as empty abstractions. The essence is not elsewhere, but here, offering itself to the gaze of anyone with eyes to see. Plato "could never, poor fellow, have seen a bunch of flowers shining with their own inner light and all but quivering under the pressure of the significance with which they were charged; could never have perceived that what rose and iris and carnation so intensely signified was nothing less than what they were—a transience that was eternal life, a perpetual perishing that was at the same time pure Being, a bundle of minute, unique particulars in which, by some unspeakable yet self-evident paradox, was to be seen the divine source of all existence."[15]

The folds in the draperies and in his trousers become "a labyrinth of endlessly significant complexity." They are nothing less than "living hieroglyphs that stand in some peculiarly expressive way for the unfathomable mystery of pure being."[16]

As for Bucke, all these impressions produce a "consciousness of the cosmos" and an "indescribable feeling of elation." Yet, for Huxley, another feeling creeps in, one which will later open a transition toward the mysticism of Mallarmé. It is a feeling not of exaltation or joy, although these are present in abundance, but of fear and desperation. Here is his account of his state of mind as he turned his eyes to a chair on the patio of his apartment: "Confronted by a chair which looked like a Last Judgement . . . , which, after a long time and considerable difficulty I recognized as a chair, I found myself all at once on the brink of panic. This, I suddenly felt, was going too far. Too far, even though the going was into deeper beauty, deeper significance. The fear, as I analyze it in retrospect, was of being overwhelmed, *of disintegrating under a pressure of reality greater than a mind accustomed to living most of the time in a cozy world of symbols could possibly bear.*"[17]

The italics above, which are mine, stress a sense of fear, of terror, at the prospect of losing control of one's mind. This fear, this feeling of impending psychic disintegration, is an aspect of mystical experience we have not encountered so far. It is usually associated with another, more profound kind of mystical insight, one which seems to work more fundamental and permanent changes on the psyche of the mystic. Huxley stopped short of his terror. Others will pass on through.

The following experience, recorded by John Addington Symonds, is transitional as well. For Symonds, to a much greater degree than for Huxley, the basic insight brings on a sense of dread:

> Suddenly, at church, or in company, or when I was reading . . . I felt the approach of the mood. Irresistibly it took possession of my mind and will, lasted what seemed an eternity, and disappeared in a series of rapid sensations which resembled the awakening from anesthetic influence. One reason I disliked this kind of trance was that I could not describe it to myself.
>
> I cannot even now find words to render it intelligible. It consisted in a gradual but swiftly progressive obliteration of space, time, sensation, and the multitudinous factors of experience which seem to qualify what we are pleased to call our Self. In proportion as these conditions of ordinary consciousness were subtracted, the sense of underlying or essential consciousness acquired intensity. At last nothing remained but a pure absolute, abstract Self. The universe became without form and void of content. But Self persisted, formidable in its vivid keenness, feeling the most poignant doubt about reality, ready, as it were, to find existence a bubble round about it. And what then? The apprehension of a coming dissolution, the grim conviction that this state was the last state of the conscious self, the sense that I had followed the last thread of being to the verge of the abyss, and had arrived at the demonstration of eternal Maya, of illusion, stirred or seemed to stir me up again. The return to ordinary conditions of sentient existence began by my first recovering the power of touch, and then the gradual though rapid influx of familiar impressions and diurnal interests. At last I felt myself once more a human being: and though the riddle of what is meant by life remained unsolved, I was thankful for this return from the abyss—this deliverance from so awful an initiation into the mysteries of scepticism.[18]

Symonds makes clear the way in which the mystic state can be a source of terror as well as inspiration. The unitary vision, most often bringing an irresistible sense of beatitude, can also, and with equal force, bring on a sense of impending loss of self in the absolute void.

This paradoxical effect led W. T. Stace, in his evaluation of reported mystical experience, to distinguish between two main types of insight, between two different "ways" which mystics have seemed to find open. The first, the one we have discussed so far and by far the most frequently encountered, he calls *extrovertive*. The other way, adumbrated by Huxley and Symonds but not really experienced by either of them, Stace calls *introvertive*.[19] This latter way is not one which opens before one suddenly and disappears just as suddenly, as in the case of N. M., for instance, or of Dr. Bucke. Nor is it gratuitous. It generally reveals itself only after a very long period of conscious or unconscious preparation of the individual psyche. Even after it does reveal itself its obscurities recede very slowly; it leads to the unitary life, to the reconciliation of opposites, only after a terrible struggle in the course of which the mystic is all but destroyed by the awful experience of the universal emptiness through which he must pass. This is the struggle, the mystic death, which Saint John of the Cross called the "dark night of the soul." William James felt justified in listing *transiency* as an almost universal characteristic of mystical experience.[20] Far from being transient, however, the introvertive experience is a slow and immensely painful cycle of destruction, death, and rebirth of the whole soul. Rather than the work of a minute or an hour, this cycle is likely to be the work of a lifetime.

In his "Treatise which deals with the manner in which a soul may prepare itself to attain to union with God," Saint John of the Cross teaches that the first step along the way is the turning away from the ordinary *affirmations* of the understanding and imagination concerning the divine nature, and the embarking on a *negative* way.[21] "God," he says, "is not comprised in any image or form, nor contained in any particular kind of knowledge . . . The soul, in order to be united with God, must not take hold of any distinct form or any particularized knowledge. . . ." The soul on the way to God "must learn to know him by what he is not rather than by what he is."[22]

After the soul has disciplined itself and cleared itself of what we have elsewhere called the "limiting categories," after it has freed itself from its "love for the things of the world and gained some spiritual strength in God, it then begins to enter into its 'noche oscura.' " For such souls God "turns all this light into darkness, shuts the open door and plugs the source of the sweet waters of the spirit. . . . He . . . leaves them in such total darkness that they do not know where to turn with their imagination and their thoughts. . . . Those spiritual things and devout exercises wherein they formerly found pleasure and delight appear to them bitter and insipid. And all this is for them a new and strange experience since everything seems to have turned into its opposite."

Speaking from his own experience, Saint John declares that God leads the soul "by the most lofty path of dark contemplation and spiritual aridity, wherein the soul believes itself to be completely lost." "As long as the aridity of this night lasts," he continues, "spiritual persons suffer great tribulations, not only on account of the aridity they experience, but also because of their fear that they have lost their way. They imagine that . . . God has abandoned them." The soul believes itself "to be perishing in a dreadful spiritual death," and that God has abandoned it and "flung it into utter darkness."[23]

For Saint John of the Cross this dark night broke finally onto the rapturous dawn of divine union. But on what dawn could it break for an atheist, for Mallarmé? Such is one major question to be answered in the course of the chapters which follow.

The extrovertive mystic looks *outward* and discovers the One in the objects of his experience. N. M. and Aldous Huxley (if we exclude his one moment of dread) afford us perfect examples of this type. The introvertive mystic, on the other hand, looks into himself and there discovers the One as an "undifferentiated unity,"[24] a void, a nothingness in which his existence is rooted but from which it, at least at the outset, can no longer draw nourishment. D. T. Suzuki, describing the Buddhist void, says that it is "Absolute emptiness . . . there is no time, no space, no becoming."[25] Except for one thing, the Buddhist experience would seem to be much like the introvertive experience we have been describing. The difference is that for the Buddhist the goal to be reached is the final extinction of individual consciousness, a giving up of the personal in the name of identification with the void. In short, Nirvana. The Westerner, however, if he is able to pass beyond the initial stage, presses on to some reconciliation wherein the individual consciousness continues to exist as a part of, yet distinguishable from, the absolute.

The introvertive experience is essentially one of psychological destruction and reconstruction of the whole mind on both its conscious and unconscious levels. The mind, having reached a point where it can no longer coherently deal with the experiences and interpretations which impose themselves upon it, is shattered by the chaotic rush of that experience. Jung has often described, in terms of his analytical theory, such psychological states. They occur, he says, when we seem "caught and entangled in aimless experience, and the judging intellect, with its categories, proves itself powerless. Human interpretation fails, for a turbulent life situation has arisen that refuses to fit any of the traditional meanings assigned to it." This failure of interpretation brings on a "moment of collapse," when one sinks into "a final death." Such a death is not a "voluntary submission and humiliation decked in moral garb, but an utter and unmistakable defeat drowned with panic fear of demoralization. Only," Jung continues, "when all the props and crutches are broken, and no cover from the rear offers the slightest hope of security does it become possible for us to experience an archetype that until then had lain hidden . . . : the archetype of meaning."[26]

There are, as we shall see further on, remarkable analogies between Jung's generalized experience and Mallarmé's particular one. But the most important thing here is simply to realize that there is an initial deeply negative stage through which the introvertive mystic passes, a stage where the soul is conscious of nothing so much as a "profound emptiness in itself" and sees in itself only "miserable imperfections, dryness and emptiness of the understanding, and abandonment of the spirit in darkness."[27] Only after the deepest awareness of the disparity between individual mind and absolute Being does the inward-looking mystic achieve that monistic insight, that union, which is glimpsed by the contemplative extrovert, at least momentarily, from the beginning. But as though in recompense, his experience is more profound, "more complete."[28] It is archetypally rooted in man's apprehension of the universal cycle of life, death and resurrection as the most fundamental expression of the limits and longings of the human condition.

To further illustrate the distinction drawn here between the two basic mystical types, let us consider for a moment Rimbaud's vision as contrasted with that of Mallarmé. To transform himself into a poète-voyant Rimbaud undertook his famous "long et raisonné dérèglement" of all the senses. This theory already points up his clearly extrovertive orientation. It is not so much within himself that he hopes to discover the "inconnu," but in the world, provided that that world can be perceived afresh, through sense organs made utterly free from the "reducing valve" effect of daily preoccupations with the practical and the useful, and from the compartmentalization of the habitually imposed system of concepts through which our knowledge of the world is usually strained. The truth about the world will then be not so much *known* as *experienced* in a confrontation of freshly cleansed perception with, as Bergson would say, "les données immédiates de la conscience."

The prose poem "Aube," for instance, records just such an experience:

J'ai embrassé l'aube d'étè.

Rien ne bougeait encore au front des palais. L'eau était morte. Les camps d'ombre ne quittaient pas la route du bois. J'ai marché, réveillant les haleines vives et tièdes, et les pierreries regardèrent, et les ailes se levèrent sans bruit.

La première entreprise fut, dans le sentier déjà rempli de frais et blêmes éclats, une fleur qui me dit son nom.

Je ris au wasserfall blond qui s'échèvela à travers les sapins: à la cime argentée je reconnus la déesse.

Alors je levai un à un les voiles. Dans l'allée, en agitant les bras. Par la plaine, où je l'ai dénoncée au coq. A la grand'ville elle fuyait parmi les clochers et les dômes, et courant comme un mendiant sur les quais de marbre je la chassais.

En haut de la route, près d'un bois de lauriers, je l'ai entourée avec ses voiles amassées, et j'ai senti un peu son immense corps. L'aube et l'enfant tombèrent au bas du bois.

Au réveil il était midi.[29]

The similarities between this vision and that of N. M., for instance, are at once apparent, although Rimbaud's goes further. In a moment of privileged perception, gratuitous for N. M., perhaps earned by Rimbaud, the objects around the poet come alive. There is darkness, then a half-light in which, Rimbaud says, "une fleur me dit son nom"; that is, a flower revealed itself in such a way as not to refer the mind back and away to the concept "flower," but to draw the mind into the heart of its own unique existence. The "voice" of the flower draws the poet into a kind of oneness with the mysterious life force, the inner core of being, which underlies and gives unity to what the rational mind would perceive as separate and distinct phenomena. This feeling of Oneness continues to impose itself until it reaches its climax and release in the coming together in mystic embrace of the poet and the dawn-goddess herself. Rimbaud has looked outward and has achieved union.

Mallarmé, on the other hand, who was much more deeply mystic than Rimbaud, is commonly reproached for his almost complete indifference to the exterior world. But, as we shall see, such a reproach betrays a fundamental misunderstanding of the quality of Mallarmé's vision. His so-called "indifference" to the natural world was not a stylistic accident nor a flaw of sensibility, but a most revealing reflection of the way in which he conceived that world. The phenomena which come to the poet from without are little more than shadows of "vaines formes de matière"[30] and serve to cover rather than discover the noumenal world. Mallarmé turned inward, and discovered there not the *plenum*, which,

in its metaphorical expression of fullness and light constitutes the universe of the extrovertive mystic, but the
vacuum, the void, the absence, and the darkness which Saint
John of the Cross had discovered before him.

Yet this void is also a unity, and if it is dark, it will
better serve to frame the brief *éclat* of beauty drawn by the
poet from his interior source, just as the night sky frames the
falling star.

Notes

1. *The Varieties of Religious Experience* (New York, 1961), p. 388.

2. Rollo May, ed., *Symbolism in Religion and Literature* (New York,
1961), p. 119.

3. *Mysticism* (New York, 1961), p. 3.

4. Quoted in W. T. Stace, *Mysticism and Philosophy* (New York,
1960), p. 196.

5. New York, 1925, p. 7.

6. Underhill, *Mysticism,* p. 3.

7. C. G. Jung, *Complete Works,* IX, Pt. 1 (New York, 1959), p. 35.

8. Stace, *Mysticism and Philosophy,* pp. 71–72.

9. *Cosmic Consciousness* (New York, 1901), pp. 3–4.

10. Quoted in James, *Varieties,* p. 306.

11. Quoted in Stace, pp. 21–22.

12. *Letters of Hart Crane,* ed. Brom Weber (New York, 1952), pp.
91–92.

13. *The Doors of Perception* (London, 1954), p. 22.

14. *Ibid.,* p. 26.

15. *Ibid.,* pp. 17–18.

16. *Ibid.,* p. 30.

17. *Ibid.,* p. 55.

18. Quoted by James H. Leuba in *The Psychology of Religious
Mysticism* (New York, 1925), p. 212.

19. *Mysticism and Philosophy,* p. 61.

20. In his *Varieties* (pp. 292–293), James lists "four marks" which
identify truly mystical experience: Ineffability, Noetic quality, Transiency,
Passivity.

21. *The Dark Night of the Soul,* trans. and ed. Kurt F. Reinhardt
(New York, 1957), p. 1.

22. *Ibid.,* pp. 63, 106.

23. *Ibid.*, pp. 171, 5, 174, 191.

24. Stace, *Mysticism and Philosophy*, p. 87.

25. Quoted by Stace, *Mysticism and Philosophy*, p. 109.

26. Jung, *Works*, IX, 35.

27. Underhill, *Mysticism*, p. 91.

28. Stace, *Mysticism and Philosophy*, p. 31.

29. Arthur Rimbaud, *Œuvres complètes* (Paris, 1954), p. 194.

30. Stéphane Mallarmé, *Propos sur la poésie* (Monaco, 1944), p. 59.

The Years of Preparation

Chapter Two

The important years in the study of the development of
Mallarmé's conception of the absolute are those which ex-
tend from his childhood to about 1870, yet no single writer
has adequately dealt with this period as a whole. One frequent error among students of Mallarmé has been to dis-
count the importance of the formative years spent at home
and in school. Few of the earlier writers go beyond Thibaudet's simple statement that "il appartenait à une bonne
et quelque peu vieille famille de bourgeoisie parisienne, de
fonctionnaires," and that, consequently, "sa vie extérieure
fut simple et unie."[1] Adile Ayda, who *does* do more, is so
impressed with what she has been able to turn up about
Mallarmé's boyhood and lycée years—which is indeed of first
importance—that she does not do justice to the changes and
developments that took place between the year of the *bacca-
lauréat* and the composition of *Igitur*.[2] Yet this latter period
is surely the one during which Mallarmé's definitive views
on the nature of the artist, his art, and the world took shape.

Thibaudet, writing eighteen years before the publication
of Mondor's *Vie de Mallarmé*, does make some comments on
what he calls Mallarmé's "idealism." It had its origin, he
says, in "un orgueil éperdu de la vie intérieure" which he—
the poet—"veut supérieur à la vie terrestre que sa nature lui
interdit."[3] And Thibaudet goes on to point out what he
considers the similarities between Mallarmé's idealism and

16

that of Schopenhauer, on whose philosophy, he says, the poetry of Mallarmé is the most striking commentary.

In making these remarks, Thibaudet is getting close to the central problem of understanding the transcendent reality which Mallarmé tries to express, but his explanation is, as might be expected given his lack of data, little more than a vague over-simplification. He does make the important point, ignored by some commentators who came after him, that Mallarmé, "par sa passion même de l'absolu, était détourné de la culture livresque,"[4] so that, although Thibaudet can find no word better suited than "idealism" to characterize Mallarmé's work, he admits that it would be an error "de relier l'idéalisme de Mallarmé à des racines philosophiques, de la rattacher à l'influence de penseurs dont il n'a sans doute rien lu."[5] But where, one would ask, does that leave Schopenhauer?

Thibaudet, comparing Baudelaire and Mallarmé, finds that the greatest weakness and limitation of both poets was that they "n'ont pu sortir d'eux-mêmes."[6] But, as we have shown, far from imposing a limitation, Mallarmé's turning inward was the very condition of his infinite mystical expansion.

Guy Delfel, who published his *L'Esthétique de Stéphane Mallarmé* in 1951, carries the theme of idealism to its ultimate conclusion. He by-passes Schopenhauer and connects Mallarmé's thought directly with that of Plato, making the poet's absolute identical with the Greek philosopher's abstract realm of Ideas. Delfel says that what Mallarmé is really trying to discover through, and embody in, his art is the transcendent world of Platonic forms. Mallarmé, says Delfel, conceived the "Idea" as a "réalité transcendante obscurément sentie dans le vie sensible."[7]

Consider, for instance, this stanza from *Prose*:

> Oui, dans une île que l'air charge
> De vue et non de visions
> Toute fleur s'étalait plus large
> Sans que nous en devisions.

Delfel's commentary is as follows: "Le paysage réel s'est effacé au profit de l'île de pures Idées. Le monde terrestre, écrit Mallarmé, est une 'simple épure d'une grandiose aquarelle,' le reflet d'un lieu 'autre part situé'. Dans cet univers platonicien, la *vue* des essences a remplacé les *visions* quotidiennes et les fleurs idéales, *plus larges,* leur réproduction d'ici-bas. Ce miracle s'est accompli en silence."[8] Delfel recognizes that Mallarmé was basically introspective. The poet, he says, discovered the essential forms within himself just as the slave boy in the *Meno* "reminisced" the proof of a geometric theorem.

L'Esthétique de Stéphane Mallarmé, like other works which try to develop a Platonic interpretation of Mallarmé's work, makes a coherent case for the point of view it represents, especially with the selective use of texts like the following one from the preface written by Mallarmé for René Ghil's *Traité du verbe.* Mallarmé speaks of the suggestive power of poetic language, and again he chooses as illustration the image of the flower: "Je dis: une fleur! et, hors de l'oubli où ma voix relègue aucun contour, en tant que quelque chose d'autre que les calices sus, musicalement se lève, idée même et suave, l'absente de tous les bouquets."[9]

Taken separately, the Platonic context of those lines seems rather clear. Such selection of texts, however, in the long run proves misleading. A close reading of *all* the texts, especially of Mallarmé's correspondence, gives indisputable grounds for refutation. Furthermore, Platonic idealism is a pluralism, achieved by raising the separate concepts, definitions, and abstractions of the mind to a metaphysical level. Such a system is quite incompatible with the monistic insight, the vision of unity which seems to be a part of all mystical experience, and which was certainly part of Mallarmé's.

Guy Michaud, in a tone much less insistent than that of Delfel, and in a book full of important insights, tries to link the Mallarméan "system" to that of Hegel. Michaud begins by wondering how "de cette vie terne et banale a pu surgir une oeuvre dont la nouveauté fit scandale et qui, dans son originalité, s'est voulue *unique.*" The answer, he says, safely enough, lies in Mallarmé's "biographie intérieure." **This** biography he proceeds to outline in a sketchy summary full of rather superficial conjecture. The years of Mallarmé's adolescence are quickly passed over: "Rien dans son enfance ni dans son adolescence ne semblait promettre Stéphane Mallarmé à une destinée singulière." Michaud considers that conflicts at school were largely responsible for the development of Mallarmé's pensive, withdrawn nature. When he was ten, he was sent "en pension" to a school in Auteuil, where, forced to mix with the "fils de haute société" on a footing less than equal, he developed an inferiority complex and an introspective turn of mind. "Il demande déjà," observes Michaud, "au rêve l'évasion d'un monde hostile."[10] Michaud merely notes in passing the death of Maria, twelve-year-old sister of the poet, during Mallarmé's own fifteenth year. He does not offer any comment.

The next important date in this psychological biography, continues Michaud, is the year 1861, the year when Mallarmé discovered Baudelaire.[11] "Le paysage baudelairien," Michaud explains, "répond bien à un tempérament rêveur, mélancolique, mystique." The prose poem "Plainte d'automne" was written under this new inspiration. According to Michaud, it was from Baudelaire that Mallarmé learned "le prix de la densité et de la conception." And, more important, under Baudelaire's tutelage Mallarmé began to become conscious of the " 'double postulation' qui lui aussi le déchire: la hantise de la mort et la soif d'idéal."[12]

According to Michaud, there remained to complete the formation of Mallarmé's inner self only the experience of the middle and late sixties. Michaud, however, does not follow the development nor show the extreme duration of the crisis. He is most interested in interpreting it in Hegelian terms. He points out that Mallarmé knew Hegel principally through his friend, Eugène Lefébure, and that it was precisely with this friend that he visited at Cannes during the general time when, according to his correspondence, he made his discovery of Nothingness. "Hegel," Michaud says, "révèle à Mallarmé . . . que le Néant n'est pas un aboutissement mais un point de départ, et que ce Néant, ce Non-Etre, n'est autre que l'Être-même en son premier état."[13]

Adile Ayda has pointed out that Michaud's "biographie intérieure" contains so many errors of fact, interpretation, and even of chronology, that one is not inclined to accept wholeheartedly its thesis on the importance for Mallarmé of Hegel's thought. In reality, Michaud, like Delfel, mentions nothing not explainable more coherently and completely in other terms, as I shall show later. Michaud's basic error has been to assume that it is necessary to refer to some fixed intellectual thought system in order to understand what Mallarmé is saying. Mallarmé did not try to make a system. He tried to communicate what had taken place within himself. To describe what he intuitively knew to be true he borrowed vocabulary and concepts from whatever sources were at hand.

The significant question is not the degree to which Mallarmé's thought may be said to be Platonic or Hegelian. Rather it is the one of determining the quality of the experience which required the use of Hegelian or Platonic terms for its description. Only in that form does the question deal with Mallarmé himself and begin to approach that incomprehensible depth of being, that welling up into consciousness of utter mystery which is at the heart of his life and work.

Adile Ayda, in her *Le drame intérieur de Mallarmé,* does, as we have indicated, pose the question in the right way. In so doing she achieves remarkable results, and for the first time throws real light on the passions and conflicts of Mallarmé's early years. Her only fault lies in stopping short and breaking off her study at too early a date.

Thibaudet had written of Mallarmé: "Rien de ce qu'il écrivit ne le montre angoissé par des problèmes religieux, et du catholicisme il n'a jamais parlé que pour en percevoir des analogies littéraires."[14] Mlle Ayda begins by taking issue with that view. On the contrary, she says, the whole of Mallarmé's youth constituted a drama which led from absolute belief, through rebellion and doubt, to final and total rejection of the catholic God of his childhood. This drama, she continues, was not played out on the margin of his life, but took place at its very center, coloring, indeed determining, the poet's future psychological development. Mlle Ayda's thesis is that no one can hope to understand Mallarmé the man without first understanding the religious and metaphysical conflicts of the youthful drama which her book attempts to reconstruct.

Drawing for the most part on the letters published by Henri Mondor in his *Mallarmé plus intime*,[15] letters exchanged between the poet, his grandparents, and his sister Maria, Mlle Ayda attempts to establish that the dominance of the introspective side of his nature, and his profound attachment to the church and its rituals, can be traced as far back as we have any real information about him. She points out that as a boy Mallarmé felt the presence of God as a "hymen mystérieux,"[16] a presence which became all the more important for him as the death of his mother and the early remarriage of his father left the poet and his sister virtual orphans, cared for by the pious maternal grandparents. "L'orphelin," writes Mlle Ayda, "vit donc dans le rêve et cette évasion dans le rêve le rend heureux: il trouve, dans le Monde Invisible bonté, pureté, harmonie, et beauté, choses par qui sa petite âme de futur poète est comblée."[17]

What Mlle Ayda has so far said cannot be absolutely proved, but from the evidence presented it is certainly an acceptable explanation of Mallarmé's state of mind at the time. But in the conclusion to this part of her argument, in her zeal to trace everything that can be found in his mature work to an early origin, she pushes her thesis too far, concluding that "L'ivresse qu'il a goûté à contempler ce monde supra-terrestre, n'est autre chose qu'une joie mystique continue." Now, there is no evidence at all, no text to support this transformation at her hands of a deep but childish piety into a "joie mystique." Piety and mysticism, while not mutually exclusive, are not at all the same thing.

Continuing her analysis, Mlle Ayda says that Mallarmé's first mystical experience coincides with the date of his first communion, in 1854. From it, she says, he derived a sense of beatitude and union which continued to grow until, in 1857, "Elle prend fin ... par un réveil, un désenivrement brusque et pénible, dont le choc laissera l'âme du poète ébranlé jusqu'à la fin de sa vie."[18] This shock was the death, on August 31, 1857, of Maria, his beloved younger sister.

Adile Ayda is one of the first writers to study the profound effect of this death on Mallarmé.[19] The death, coming just four and a half months after Maria's own first communion, tragically introduced into the poet's mind the initial seed of doubt concerning the benevolent nature of God and the harmonious working of the universe. Mallarmé described something of his reaction to Maria's death in *"Plainte d'automne,"* a prose poem written some four years later. He had withdrawn even more into himself, sought out solitude; he had a sense of the falling away of a more privileged life. "Depuis que la blanche créature n'est plus," he tells us, "étrangement et singulièrement, j'ai aimé tout ce qui se résumait en ce mot chute."[20]

This period of crisis is the same one, by the way, that Michaud would attribute to Mallarmé's inability to mix well with the "fils de riches" at the school in Auteuil. That such a superficial interpretation might even have been proposed is an indication of the great value of Mlle Ayda's study, whatever disagreements one may have with her on some matters of interpretation and scope.

The falling away from the divine which Mallarmé began to feel after the death of Maria was magnified to the point of absolute denial by the death of another girl, in 1859. This time the victim was Harriet Smythe, the daughter of an American couple who were neighbors of Mallarmé's grandparents in Passy. Mallarmé came to know Harriet Smythe during the summer of Maria's culminating crisis and death. He seems to have developed for Harriet a very deep and pure affection. Certain lines in the poems "Sa fosse est creusée" and "Sa fosse est fermée"—the one written shortly before Harriet's death and the other shortly thereafter—show that for Mallarmé Harriet was as important as Maria had been. Only two years after their meeting Harriet died of the same kind of chest ailment that had killed Maria. This second crisis had, as we have said, the effect of turning the already doubting poet definitively away from the God he had adored: Mlle Ayda points to lines in "Sa fosse est creusée" which "translate" as

> Je voudrais retrouver le bonheur et la foi
> Mais si Harriet meurt je ne le pourrai pas.

If Harriet dies, Mallarmé says, "je maudirai."

From this time on, all that remains of God in his work will be the secularized, depersonalized *Azur,* serene and ironic in its indifference to the misfortunes of those below. The whole of Mallarmé's mature work, concludes Mlle Ayda, will consist in attempts to reestablish, or, rather, to find a suitable substitute for the "vieux rêve," the transcendent harmony he had felt as a boy and then lost.

The first crisis, coming to its final climax in 1859, is in Mlle Ayda's eyes "non seulement la première, mais la plus importante, puisque . . . elle a donné naissance à toutes les autres."[21] While not denying the great importance of what Mlle Ayda has to tell us, we would conclude that what she has described remains only an important preliminary stage in Mallarmé's development, and not, as she claims, the crucial one. The crisis she describes seems to have taken place on a wholly rational, intellectual plane. It is that of a human ego which denies God after having understood the reality and implications of the problem of evil, and which afterwards feels a quite normal sense of loss.

Rather than being the most important stage in Mallarmé's development, this last crisis was a stage of clearing away, of preparing the ground for the "dark night" of the sixties and the final illumination which will come out of it.

Notes

1. Albert Thibaudet, *La poésie de Stéphane Mallarmé* (Paris, 1926), p. 16.

2. Adile Ayda, *Le drame intérieur de Mallarmé* (Istanbul, 1955).

3. Thibaudet, p. 98.

4. Ibid., p. 26.

5. Ibid., p. 97.

6. Ibid., p. 31.

7. Paris, 1951, pp. 35–36.

8. Guy Delfel, *Mallarmé, pages choisies* (Paris, 1954), p. 61.

9. Ibid., p. 16.

10. Guy Michaud, *Mallarmé, l'homme et l'œuvre* (Paris, 1953), p. 3 ff.

11. Adile Ayda has shown that Mallarmé had, at a considerably earlier time, copied verses of Baudelaire into one of his schoolboy notebooks.

12. Michaud, *Mallarmé,* pp. 10, 11.

13. Ibid., p. 56.

14. Poésies, p. 86.

15. Henri Mondor, *Mallarmé plus intime* (Paris, 1944).

16. Stéphane Mallarmé, *Œuvres complètes* (Paris, 1951), p. 30.

17. Drame, p. 28.

18. Ibid., p. 31.

19. The other writer one thinks of is Charles Mauron, whose *Introduction à la psychanalyse de Mallarmé* (Neûchatel, 1950) is a fascinating explanation in Freudian terms of M.'s psychological development.

20. Œuvres, p. 270.

21. Drame, p. 77.

Palingenesis

By the early 1860s, then, Mallarmé had passed from an attitude of personal anger directed against an equally personal, malevolent deity to one of alternate seeking after and despairing of an ideal, impersonal reality—serene, ironic, oppressing—from which he felt himself hopelessly removed. This is a period of exile. It is the time of his "first manner," his Baudelairean period. "Les fenêtres," "L'Azur," "Las de l'amer repos," "Brise marine," and others of his finest lyrics date from this period. Their constant theme is that of exile from the *Azur* and evasion of its gaze.

On the other hand, after 1870, the Mallarmé we know is no longer the anguished outsider, but the calm, oracular visionary, confident that he has achieved ultimate insight into the nature of Being itself. The only torment of this later period will be that of inventing and mastering a poetic vocabulary and technique commensurate with his vision.

What happened in the years between? How did the exile become a citizen of the kingdom? His correspondence for 1864–1870 answers the question. In London he had already complained to a friend of "une stérilité curieuse" which the new season, Spring, seemed to have settled upon him.[2] In France again, in 1864, from Tournon, where he had gone to begin his career as professor of English, he wrote to Albert Collignon: ". . . je ne saurais vous dire comme cette plume, abandonnée sur ma table que revêt la poussière, me semble lourde à reprendre, même pour vous écrire."[3] He suffers from headaches so severe that it seems he is losing his mind: "Quant à moi . . . je suis si souffrant du cerveau, que je deviendrais *idiot,* sans plaisanterie, si je ne respirais un meilleur air."[4]

Nevertheless, once settled in Tournon he begins work on his *Hérodiade,* a work which he feels will open new doors, and which will demand a new conception of the poet's art and a new language. Here is his letter of October 1864 to Henri Cazalis:

> . . . Pour moi, me voici résolument à l'oeuvre. J'ai enfin commencé mon Hérodiade. Avec terreur, car j'invente une langue qui doit nécessairement jaillir d'une poétique très nouvelle, que je pourrais définir en ces deux mots: *Peindre, non la chose, mais l'effet qu'elle produit.*
>
> Le vers ne doit donc pas, là, se composer de mots mais d'intentions et toutes les paroles s'éffacer devant la sensation. Je ne sais pas si tu me devines, mais j'espère que tu m'approuveras quand j'aurai réussi. Car *je veux* pour la première fois de ma vie *réussir.* Je ne toucherais jamais plus à ma plume si j'étais terrassé.[5]

He commits himself totally to this new work, which seems to offer the opportunity and impose the obligation of achieving the ultimate goal, not only of his own poetry but of *any* poetry. For a long time he is not able fully to grasp the complexity and mysterious depth of his subject. For years, literally, he will do no better than to follow it wherever it leads. In writing his work he is very much like the heroine herself, who tells the old nurse,

"J'attends une chose inconnue."

The subject resists; the poem refuses to be written. Mallarmé is often forced to abandon his work, to admit defeat. In December of 1864 he again writes to Cazalis:

> Pour les vers, je suis fini, je crois: il y a de grandes lacunes dans mon cerveau qui est devenu incapable d'une pensée suivie et

d'application. J'expie cruellement, toi seul le sais, mon ami, le
priapisme de ma jeunesse. Oui, je me regarde avec frayeur,
comme une ruine: dans toutes mes lettres, je vais mentir à mes
amis et leur dire que je travaille—mais cela n'est pas vrai.[6]

He is empty, powerless; his inspiration has deserted him;
he is on the verge of insanity. Nor can he see any hope for
the future. He holds himself in such contempt that he consciously avoids any mirror which might reflect his "face dé-
gradée et éteinte." The bitter winter in Tournon matches
his mood:

> Je suis triste. Un vent glacial et noir m'empêche de me prome-
> ner, et je ne sais que faire à la maison quand mon pauvre
> cerveau m'interdit le travail. Puis j'ai le dégoût de moi: je
> recule devant les glaces, en voyant ma face dégradée et éteinte,
> et pleure quand je me sens vide et ne puis jeter un mot sur
> mon papier implacablement blanc. Être un vieillard fini, à
> vingt-trois ans, alors que tous ceux qu'on aime vivent dans la
> lumière et les fleurs, à l'âge des chefs-d'oeuvre.[7]

His youth, he feels, is gone, and with it his genius. He is in
the desert of the spirit; he is "an old man, in a dry month
. . . waiting for rain."

Mallarmé writes to Cazalis: "Ma plume seule écrit en ce
moment, je m'ennuie à ne plus pouvoir penser."[8] And again:
". . . mon cerveau, désagrégé et noyé dans un crépuscule
aqueux, me défend l'art. Cette lettre même que je t'écris avec
tant de peine, je la quitte et la reprends après chaque phrase,
tant je suis incapable d'une application même frivole."[9]

In June of 1865 Mallarmé finally put aside *Hérodiade*—
"cette oeuvre solitaire" —which, he says, "m'avait stérilisé."
He took up another work, "un intermède héroïque, dont le
héros est un faune," which after ten years of development
would finally become *L'Après-midi d'un faune*.[10] When winter returned, however, he went back to the cold princess and
to his torment. On the fifth of December he writes: "J'ai
souffert toute la semaine d'une atroce névralgie qui battait à
mes tempes et tordait les nerfs de mes dents, le jour et la
nuit: aux minutes de répit, je me jetais en maniaque

désespéré sur une insaisissable ouverture de mon poème qui chante en moi, mais que je ne puis noter."[11] He is still waiting for the "chose inconnue," but mysterious melodies have begun to make themselves heard within him. He needs absolute solitude, he writes Aubanel, "pour entendre chanter en moi certaines notes mystérieuses."[12]

Mallarmé makes a supreme effort to capture these notes, these "impressions extra-terrestres."[13] But as he digs deeper and deeper into each line and each word, suddenly, behind and beneath his whole work and himself he discovers the opening of a double abyss. In March of 1866 he writes to Cazalis:

> ... en creusant le vers à ce point, j'ai rencontré deux abîmes, qui me désespèrent. L'un est le Néant, auquel je suis arrivé sans connaître le Bouddhisme et je suis encore trop désolé pour pouvoir croire même à ma poésie et me remettre au travail, que cette pensée écrasante m'a fait abandonner.
>
> Oui, *je le sais,* nous ne sommes que de vaines formes de matière, —mais bien sublimes pour avoir inventé Dieu et notre âme. Si sublimes, mon ami! que je veux me donner ce spectacle de la matière, ayant conscience d'être, et cependant, s'élançant forcément dans le rêve qu'elle sait n'être pas, chantant l'Âme et toutes les divines impressions pareilles qui se sont amassées en nous depuis les premiers âges, et proclamant, devant le Rien qui est la vérité, ces glorieux mensonges.[14]

The immediate consequences of his discovery seem to have been salutary. In May he is able to write: "Je suis en train de jeter les fondements d'un livre sur le Beau. Mon esprit se meut dans l'Éternel, et en a eu plusieurs frissons, si l'on peut parler ainsi de l'Immuable. Je me repose à l'aide de trois courts poèmes mais qui seront inouïs, tous trois à la glorification de la Beauté, et auxquels même, sert de repos un nombre égal de singuliers poèmes en prose. Voilà mon été. ..."[15]

The summer of 1866, then, is one of considerable enthusiasm. Certain aspects of his vision are already beginning to take shape although the peak of the crisis will not occur until the following winter. In July Mallarmé writes to Cazalis: "Je te dirai que depuis un mois je meus dans les plus purs glaciers de l'esthétique—qu'après avoir trouvé le Néant j'ai trouvé le Beau."[16] And in the same month, to Aubanel: "J'ai jeté les fondements d'une oeuvre magnifique. Tout homme a un secret à lui. Beaucoup meurent sans l'avoir trouvé, et ne le trouveront pas, parce que, morts, il n'existera plus, ni eux. Je suis mort et ressuscité avec la clef de pierreries de ma dernière cassette spirituelle. A moi maintenant de l'ouvrir en l'absence de toute impression empruntée, et son mystère s'émanera en un fort beau ciel."[17]

A week later there is another letter to Aubanel, this time with a somewhat fuller explanation:

> J'ai voulu te dire tout simplement que je venais de jeter le plan de mon oeuvre entière, après avoir trouvé la clef de moi-même, clef de voûte, ou centre, si tu veux, pour ne pas nous brouiller de métaphores,—centre de moi-même, où je me tiens comme une araignée sacrée, sur les principaux fils déjà sortis de mon esprit, et à l'aide desquels je tisserai *aux points de rencontre* de merveilleuses dentelles, que je devine, et qui existent déjà dans le sein de la Beauté. . . . Que je prévois qu'il me faudra vingt ans pour ces cinq livres dont se composera l'Oeuvre, et que j'attendrai, ne lisant qu'à mes amis comme toi, des fragments, —et me moquant de la gloire comme d'une niaiserie usée. Qu'est une immortalité relative, et se passant souvent dans l'esprit d'imbéciles, à côté de la joie de contempler l'Éternité, et d'en jouir, vivant, en soi.[18]

Of the winter which follows, that of 1866–1867, we have no letters. Mallarmé seems to have done very little writing of any kind. He was so overcome, so utterly overwhelmed by his experience that he was unable to write about it. It was deeper than any other, and finally decisive. Only after he has passed through it, in May of 1867, will he write to Cazalis that he is "non plus le Stéphane que tu as connu, —mais une aptitude qu'a l'Univers Spirituel à se voir et à se développer, à travers ce qui fut moi." He is beyond time and beyond space, an impersonal reflection of the absolute:

> Je viens de passer une année effrayante; ma Pensée s'est pensée et est arrivée à une Conception Pure. Tout ce que, par contre-coup, mon être a souffert, pendant cette longue agonie, est inénarrable, mais heureusement, je suis parfaitement mort, et la

région la plus impure où mon Esprit puisse s'aventurer est l'Éternité, mon Esprit, ce solitaire habituel de sa propre pureté que n'obscurcit plus même le reflet du Temps.

Malheureusement, j'en suis arrivé là par une horrible sensibilité, et il est temps que je l'enveloppe d'une indifférence extérieure, qui remplacera pour moi la force perdue. J'en suis, après une synthèse suprême, à cette lente aquisition de la force —incapable tu le vois, de me distraire. —Mais combien plus je l'étais, il y a plusieurs mois, d'abord dans ma lutte avec ce vieux et méchant plumage, terrassé, heureusement, Dieu. Mais même cette lutte s'était passée sur son aile osseuse, qui par une agonie plus vigoureuse que je ne l'eusse soupçonné chez lui, m'avait emporté dans les Ténèbres, je tombai, victorieux, éperdument et infiniment—jusqu'à ce qu'enfin, je me sois revu un jour devant la glace de Venise, tel que je m'étais oublié plusieurs mois auparavant. J'avoue du reste mais à toi seul, que j'ai encore besoin, tant ont été grandes les avanies de mon triomphe, de me regarder dans cette glace pour penser, et que si elle n'était pas devant la table où j'écris cette lettre, je redeviendrais le Néant. C'est t'apprendre que je suis maintenant impersonnel, et non plus le Stéphane que tu as connu, —mais une aptitude qu'a l'Univers Spirituel à se voir et à se développer, à travers ce qui fut moi.

Fragile, comme est mon apparition terrestre, je ne puis subir que les développements absolument nécessaires pour que l'Univers retrouve, en ce moi, son identité. Ainsi, je viens, à l'heure de la Synthèse, de délimiter l'oeuvre qui sera l'image de ce développement. Trois poèmes en vers, dont *Hérodiade* est l'ouverture, mais d'une pureté que l'homme n'a pas atteinte —et n'atteindra peut-être jamais, car il se pourrait que je fusse le jouet d'une illusion, et que la machine humaine ne soit pas assez parfaite pour arriver à de tels résultats. Et quatre poèmes en prose, sur la conception spirituelle du Néant. Il me faut dix ans: les aurai-je? . . . ce ne serait pas sans un serrement de coeur réel que j'entrerais dans la Disparition suprême, si je n'avais pas fini mon oeuvre, qui est l'Œuvre. Le Grand'Œuvre, comme disaient les alchimistes, nos ancêtres.[19]

In another letter, dating from the twenty-fourth of September of the same year, Mallarmé describes this same experience to Villiers de l'Isle-Adam. Four months after the May letter, the key words are the same:

Ma pensée a été jusqu'à se penser elle-même et n'a plus la force d'évoquer en un Néant unique le vide désséminé en sa porosité.

J'avais, à la faveur d'une grande sensibilité, compris la corre-
lation intime de la Poésie avec l'Univers, et, pour qu'elle fût
pure, conçu le dessein de la sortir du rêve et du hasard et de la
juxtaposer à la conception de l'univers. Malheureusement, âme
organisée simplement pour la jouissance poétique, je n'ai pu,
. . . comme vous, disposer d'un esprit. —et vous serez terrifié
d'apprendre que je suis arrivé à l'idée de l'Univers par la seule
sensation, (et que, par exemple, pour garder une notion in-
effaçable du Néant pur, j'ai dû imposer à mon cerveau la sensation du vide absolu.) Le miroir qui m'a réfléchi l'Être a été le
plus souvent l'Horreur et vous devinez si j'expie cruellement ce
diamant des Nuits innomées.

Il me reste la délimitation parfaite et le rêve intérieur de
deux livres à la fois nouveaux et éternels, l'un tout absolu
"Beauté," l'autre personnel, les "allégories somptueuses du
Néant" mais (dérision et torture de Tantale), l'impuissance de les
écrire—d'ici à bien longtemps, si mon cadavre doit ressusciter. . . .

Vraiment, j'ai peur de commencer (quoique, certes,
l'Éternité ait scintillé en moi et dévoré la notion survivant du
temps) par où notre pauvre et sacré Baudelaire a fini. . . .[20]

He was afraid to begin, and yet he did begin. And the
rest of his life was spent in the accomplishment of that Great
Work. In a later letter to Cazalis, thinking back over the
years he has just passed, he sums up: "La première phase de
ma vie a été finie. La conscience, excédée d'ombres, se ré-
veille, lentement, formant un homme nouveau, et doit
retrouver mon rêve. . . ."[21] After this date, 1869, there are no
more references in the correspondence we possess to other
experiences of this kind. He has become a new man; he has
known moments in eternity. Cazalis, answering his letter,
writes: "Mon ami, j'ai pleuré en lisant ta lettre, pleuré non
pas de te voir mort, puisque ta mort t'a fait monter dans la
vie, dans le ciel tranquil où tu rêvais d'entrer, mais pleuré
de respect et d'admiration. Tu es le plus grand poète de
ton temps, Stéphane, sache-le; et si haut que tu sois, que cet
hommage console en toi ce qui reste d'humain."[22]

It seems very clear that what Mallarmé has described in
these letters is a passage through a spiritual dark night to
rebirth as a visionary. Looking back, one may single out five
successive stages in his rebirth cycle:

1. A falling away from the divine after the deaths of Maria and Harriet Smythe ("Plainte d'automne").

2. A period of exile, Baudelairean in its hopeless longing for union ("L'Azur," "Brise marine").

3. Mysterious stirrings from within. Melodies which he cannot seem to capture, messages too difficult to decipher. A time of desperate effort to comprehend what needs to be said and the poetic necessary to say it (*Hérodiade* begun).

4. The effort, almost crushing, the passing beyond the brink of the abyss, and the falling into the heart of darkness. Reconciliation with his vision of Nothingness as ultimate reality.

5. The "new man" reenters the realm of time to fulfill his mission. He is an "aptitude qu'a l'univers spirituel à se voir." He projects the Great Work. He is a visionary. He does not seek, he has found.

Notes

1. Mallarmé, *Propos*, p. 87.
2. *Ibid.*, p. 31.
3. *Ibid.*, p. 36.
4. *Ibid.*, p. 41.
5. *Ibid.*, pp. 43–44.
6. *Ibid.*, p. 46.
7. *Ibid.*, p. 47.
8. *Ibid.*, p. 49.
9. *Ibid.*, p. 50.
10. *Ibid.*, p. 50.
11. *Ibid.*, p. 56.
12. *Ibid.*, p. 57.
13. *Ibid.*, p. 58.
14. *Ibid.*, p. 59.
15. *Ibid.*, p. 67.
16. *Ibid.*, p. 68.
17. *Ibid.*, p. 69.
18. *Ibid.*, pp. 70–71.

19. *Ibid.*, pp. 77–80.

20. A. W. Raitt, "Autour d'une lettre de Mallarmé," *Autour du symbolisme* (Paris, 1955), pp. 146–147.

21. *Propos,* p. 87.

22. Michaud, *Mallarmé,* p. 66.

The Poetic of the Ineffable

Chapter Four | *En présence de l'oeuvre belle,*
l'intelligence jouit sans discours.

—Jacques Maritain

When William James says that *ineffability* is one of the four
virtually universal marks of mystical experience,[1] the testimony of the mystics themselves certainly bears him out. For
Plotinus, ". . . the vision baffles telling"; for Eckhart, "The
mystery . . . was ineffable"; Bucke found his experience "im-
possible to describe"; Symonds "could not find words to
render it [his experience] intelligible."[2] Such a list could be
extended almost at will. One thinks of the brilliant Pascal,
who was reduced to scribbling a few disjointed phrases onto
a piece of paper which he then sewed into the lining of his
coat. Or of St. Thomas Aquinas who, weighing the tomes of
his *Summa* against ineffable knowledge of God, found them
"not worth a straw."

Guy Delfel considers it the original poetic contradiction
"de ne pas pouvoir exprimer l'éternel que par la matière,
l'extra-terrestre que par l'image et la figure."[3] He may be
right. Is it at all possible to translate a kind of knowledge
which is non-temporal and non-spatial into terms of a language which by its physical and syntactical nature can exist
only in space and time? Does language reject the mystical just
as the human body rejects a graft of foreign tissue?

34

Shelley says that

> The One remains, the many change and pass;
> Heaven's light forever shines, Earth's shadows fly;
> Life, like a dome of many colored glass,
> Stains the white radiance of Eternity . . .

The One is the transcendent purity which yet contains all possibilities, as white light contains the spectrum of color. Can physical language ever be so manipulated as to refocus the diverse colors into their original purity? Or must it always remain the staining dome, and accomplish further refraction? In short, is the conflict which, in the words of Jacques Maritain, exists "entre la transcendance de la beauté et l'étroitesse matérielle de l'oeuvre à faire,"[4] in any way reconcilable?

The primal fall from Edenic unity resulted in a fragmentation of consciousness and, consequently, of language—the tool with which consciousness interprets itself and the world. *Le Verbe,* as Mallarmé would say, is lost; all that remain are the several "langues imparfaites" of the marketplace. "La diversité, sur terre, des idiomes," Mallarmé thinks, "empêche personne de proférer les mots qui, sinon se trouveraient, par une frappe unique, elle-même matériellement la vérité."[5] The task of the poet-mystic, as Hart Crane said, may indeed be to

> String some constant harmony.

But he must do the job with a broken or imperfect instrument.

One can seriously ask if it were not better to leave the experience itself intact, to refuse to risk obscuring it by raising upon it a structure of words. Is not

> . . . le vide papier que la blancheur défend

more eloquent—and more pure—than anything written on it could ever be? Mallarmé felt very keenly that to write at all was, in a sense, to risk drawing a limit to infinity, and therefore a kind of sin against the absolute. No poem, he feared, could possibly be as expansive as the experience which inspired it. The poet's inkwell, itself "cristal comme une conscience," contains within it "sa goutte de ténèbres."[6] Yet it is with these shadows that the poet must work. To Daudet's mocking question "si c'est volontairement que vous êtes retiré dans les ténèbres . . . ou bien si c'est involontairement," Mallarmé replied: "Mais est-ce que l'opération même d'écrire n'est pas de mettre du noir sur du blanc?"[7] And again, in another place: "on n'écrit pas, lumineusement, sur champs obscur, l'alphabet des astres . . . ; l'homme poursuit noir sur blanc."[8]

From the very beginning, then, of the act of writing, the poet is struggling to redeem, by some magic, the natural opacity of and impurity of language. The first black mark on the white page is a movement *away* from that vision which constitutes the poet's essential "letter to the world." From that initial admission of failure—failure insofar as he has not been able to utter the perfect *Verbe*—the poet must go on to spin out of himself some pattern of sound, image and rhythm, some analogy which will serve as the objective emblem of his subjective conviction. He must embody the truth that he cannot rationally "explain." He must utter the unutterable. But how?

Any technique that will serve this transcendent end of art is admissible. Mallarmé's concern is not, simply, communication, but a certain *kind* of communication, the communication of an ineffable, uniquely, and supremely meaningful quality of a subjective experience. If he turns to what others—Daudet, for instance—consider inexcusable obscurity of expression, it is because that is exactly what is required by the nature of his vision. For Mallarmé, Proust's maxim is absolutely true—that style is a quality of vision.

Mallarmé, of course, had from the time of his earliest mature work considered that certain obscurity should veil the poem from any vulgar gaze and so preserve its purity. Consider, for instance, this observation: "Toute chose sacrée et qui veut demeurer sacrée s'enveloppe de mystère. Les religions se retranchent à l'abri d'arcanes dévoilés au seul prédestiné: l'art a les siens."[9] But these words from "Hérésie artistique," written in 1862, do nothing more than give voice to a youthful and somewhat snobbish aestheticism. The obscurity of his mature work comes from an infinitely more profound source: his struggle with the ineffable.

Mallarmé's first rule in the poetic of the ineffable is simply this: that suggestion works better than explanation. The reason is easy to see. Explanation operates on the level of the intellect, and is discursive; it leads at best to philosophy. Suggestion, on the other hand, bypasses the intellectual "reducing valve." It does not relate an idea to the reader, but engenders an experience within him. Suggestion is a kind of magic: "Je dis qu'existe entre les vieux procédés et le sortilège, que restera la poésie, une parité secrète. . . . Evoquer, dans une ombre exprès, l'objet tu, par des mots allusifs, jamais directs, se réduisant à du silence égal, comporte tentative proche de créer: vraisemblablement dans la limite de l'idée mis en jeu par l'enchanteur de lettres jusqu'à ce que, certes, scintille, quelque illusion égale au regard. Le vers, trait incantatoire."[10]

To name a thing is to lead away from the unique reality at hand, the living presence, and into the more familiar field of concepts and definitions by which we normally order our thoughts and reduce our perceptions to their most common and most useful denominators. Proust, transfixed before the hawthorns, felt deeper reality beneath that conceptual surface. One of the deepest currents in modern art since romanticism has been the attempt to uncover and communicate that deeper reality. What else is art for, says Mallarmé: "A quoi bon la merveille de transposer un fait de nature en sa presque disparition vibratoire selon le jeu de la parole, cependant; si ce n'est qu'en émane, sans le gêne d'un proche ou concret rappel, la notion pure."[11]

How then to proceed? Mallarmé believed that a certain vagueness of language and deliberate blurring of the outlines of sense and image so free the mind of the reader that he is able to look *into* and *through* rather than *at* a poem. The indefinite article or adjective is always preferred. Mallarmé does not speak of this particular flower or that one, but of "a" flower; not of "le baume rare émané par mensonge," but of "quelque baume rare," etc. "Pas la couleur, rien que la nuance," says Verlaine. Mallarmé agrees. But the end he is working for—the transmutation of the consciousness of the reader—is magical as well as musical.

Mallarmé uses the physical presence of words to evoke their contrary: the nothingness and silence of the introspective void. All of his later verse, whatever the subject at hand, is charged not only with indefinite modifiers where a definite one might be expected, but also with language evocative of absence, emptiness, silence, and negation. Valéry, when he first read Mallarmé, felt a kind of occult communication from the verses although he did not in any normal sense "understand" them. The mere sound, the suggestiveness of the words, their semantic aura, produced in him, as he says, a rather "cabbalistic" sensation of profundity. Much of this mysteriously immediate communication depends upon the play of negatives. It is as though

Deep in the mind, far back,

the terms of absence and negation open a space in the reader's consciousness where the ineffable experience of the poet is recreated and relived. The intensity of immediate experience is the quality which first attracts one to Mallarmé's verse. In the beginning, what one feels far exceeds in meaningfulness what one understands. This initial experience may lead to an effort at exegesis, to a search for total rational comprehension. But such comprehension, even when achieved, seldom—one is tempted to say never—heightens the subjective state of consciousness, the all-important "suggestion," which was first called up in the mind by the poem. Indeed it may even dissipate it.

There is an anecdote which illustrates in a delicate way the Mallarméan touch. Léopold Dauphin recalls "un soir d'automne où nous nous promenions en canot." He is talking to Mallarmé of his own verses:

J'en ai fait deux hier, lui dis-je. Je
m'adresse aux raisins vendangés.

"Vous ne griserez plus au soir
l'aile si blonde de l'abeille."

Il tire une bouffée de sa pipe, fait gonfler
la voile, donne un coup au barre; je
crois qu'il ne m'a pas entendu et je vais
lui redire les vers quand j'entends:

"Vous ne griserez aucun soir
L'aile blonde aussi de l'abeille."

J'étais ravi. . . .[12]

The change in wording is slight. Yet, as unimportant as this
bit of verse is, it gains considerably in depth through this
transformation into Mallarméan terms, playing on the ambi-
guity of the negative "aucun" and on the analogy suggested
by the use of "aussi."

What Mallarmé accomplishes is not so much a transformation of the object itself as of the quality of consciousness
which apprehends it. And for this new consciousness, the object becomes, in its magic absence-in-presence, an upsurge
into experience of absolute Being, mutely offering itself for
our contemplation.

Almost every poem of Mallarmé contains examples of the
kind of language we are discussing. Let us take, for instance,
the first two lines of "Salut":

Rien, cette écume, vierge vers
A ne désigner que la coupe. . . .

The first word of this miniature *art poétique, rien,* stands
alone, in its own place, set off from the rest of the line, and
indeed from the rest of the poem, by a comma. Its effect is
heightened by the echoes it finds in *écume* (transient, mere
nothing), *vièrge* (absence of the lover), and *coupe* (the
empty vessel). This poem, proffering its affirmation of nothingness, was written in 1893 and was to stand at the head of

the complete *Poésies* which Mallarmé was preparing at the time of his death.

Again, consider "Une dentelle s'abolit":

> Une dentelle s'abolit
> Dans le doute du Jeu suprême
> A n'entr'ouvrir comme un blasphême
> Qu'absence éternelle de lit.
>
> Cet unanime blanc conflit
> D'une guirlande avec la même,
> Enfui contre la vitre blême
> Flotte plus qu'il n'ensevelit.
>
> Mais, chez qui du rêve se dore
> Tristement dort une mandore
> Au creux néant musicien
>
> Telle que vers quelque fenêtre
> Selon nul ventre que le sien,
> Filial on aurait pu naître.

Quite apart from any literal "sense" one might feel obliged to assign—or refuse to assign—to these lines, there is an accumulation of negation (s'abolit, doute, absence éternelle, blanc, blême, creux néant) which has an effect of its own. This effect leads in the third stanza to the introduction of

> . . . une mandore
> Au creux néant musicien.

and in the last stanza to "quelque fenêtre" (which one? perhaps some interior one of the mind) and "nul ventre." Reading through, then, in an attitude totally open to suggestion, one has a vague impression of a room, a window at which a delicate white curtain is blowing in a light breeze, and, perhaps, of the presence of the poet. All else is calm, night, and silence.

That is all a first reading reveals, but it is *enough;* one knows more than one can say if, as Mallarmé hoped, one feels the utter mystery of mind existent in the universal void. Exegesis, we will repeat, may add to comprehension, but cannot make more complete or more intense the kind of knowledge (experience) we are talking about here, the only kind of any importance for Mallarmé.

The "creux néant musicien," symbolizing the nothingness which yet engenders the poem, brings to mind an earlier work which treats the relationship between poetic utterance and the quality of silence, the poem *Sainte*.

> A la fenêtre recélant
> Le santal vieux qui se dédore
> De sa viole étincelant
> Jadis avec flûte ou mandore,
>
> Est la Sainte pâle, étalant
> Le livre vieux qui se déplie
> Du Magnificat ruisselant
> Jadis selon vêpre et complie:
>
> A ce vitrage d'ostensoir
> Que frôle une harpe par l'Ange
> Formée avec son vol du soir
> Pour la délicate phalange
>
> Du doigt que, sans le vieux santal
> Ni le vieux livre, elle balance
> Sur le plumage instrumental,
> Musicienne du silence.

This is surely one of Mallarmé's most eloquently simple poems. As C. F. MacIntyre points out, its real theme is that of "an unplayed chord on an unplayable instrument."[13] The movement and imagery are carefully balanced, turning on the colon which punctuates the last line of the second stanza as a diptych might turn on a hinge. In this poem there is neither sound nor motion, and in that sense it is a denial of space; the words *vieux* and *jadis,* used twice, and the image of the Saint herself, turn the mind away from the present and dislocate the sense of time. The first two stanzas depict instruments, old and no longer used, which once made music. Now a subtler music is called for: those unheard melodies which, for Keats, were sweeter. It's a music of restraint. The Saint's finger is posed on the harp-shaped wing, forever. It will never move, nor the harp play. But that very restraint, that absence of any sensible vibration, calls up in the soul of the reader those very notes which can never be played, the ones which Mallarmé heard within himself.

Poems like these communicate that which cannot be said precisely by not saying it. In their silence and hieroglyphically fixed attitudes these works are part of a spiritual *mime*. They reveal without discourse the "ontological splendor" of the mystery of Being.[14]

Notes

1. For the others see Chapter I, n. 20.

2. Stace, *Mysticism,* p. 277.

3. Delfel, *L'esthetique,* p. 58.

4. *Art et scholastique* (Paris, 1927), p. 74.

5. Mallarmé, *Œuvres,* pp. 363–364.

6. *Œuvres,* p. 370.

7. Quoted in Thibaudet, *Poésie,* p. 64.

8. *Œuvres,* p. 370.

9. *Ibid.,* p. 257.

10. *Ibid.,* p. 400.

11. *Ibid.,* p. 368.

12. Quoted in Mondor, *Vie de Mallarmé,* pp. 412–413.

13. *French Symbolist Poetry* (Berkeley, 1954), p. 130.

14. For a discussion of art as revelatory of the "ontological splendor" see Maritain, *Art et Scholastique,* p. 28.

The Poetic of Monistic Insight

/ *I have no doubt of this, that if the soul had the remotest notion of what being means she would never waver from it for an instant.*

—Meister Eckhart

Monistic insight is insight into the essential unity underlying the phenomena which ordinarily present themselves to our minds as separate, discrete events. Taken as ultimate reality these "disconnected" events would reduce our experience of the world to the chaos of disparate impressions pressing in upon us at all times. One function of scientific synthesis is to reduce these impressions into classes of experience from which it can induce the "laws of nature" which relate those classes in a mechanical way and so make some comprehension of them possible. The achievement of Newton was to work what in his time seemed the most universal synthesis possible, expressing in a single, simple formula the laws of matter and motion, that is to say, the mechanics of the universe.

When Blake said that you

> ... Believe a lie
> When you see with, not through, the eye

he was talking about physical vision as distinguished from spiritual vision. The scientist sees *with* the eye, and if what he sees is not really a lie, its truth is as superficial as it is practical. For Bacon knowledge was power. For the mystic, however, real knowledge is union with the divine, it is in-

43

sight into the unitary heart of Being, it is absolute certainty that the universe is "one single, eternal, ineffable substance."[1]

Different minds have conceived of that single substance in different ways. For Whitman, life in all things was the unifying principle. For Meister Eckhart, it was the Godhead: God, he says,

> . . . is being. . . . In being, mere being, lies all that is at all. Being is the first name. Defect means lack of being. Our whole life ought to be being. So far as our life is being, so far is it in God. So far as our life is feeble, but taking it as being, it excels anything that life can ever boast. I have no doubt of this, that if the soul had the remotest notion of what being means she would never waver from it for an instant. The most trivial thing perceived in God, a flower for example as espied in God, would be a thing more perfect than the universe. The vilest thing present in God as being is better than angelic knowledge.[2]

For Eckhart, defect, or sin, is falling away from being and as such stands between the mystic and the divine. The most urgent spiritual task is to remedy the defect and reintegrate the self into being: "God must be very I, I very God, so consummately one that this he and this I are one 'is,' in this is-ness working one work eternally."[3]

Eckhart's words are obviously translatable into non-Christian terms. When they are, a very clear statement of the mystical world-view emerges: Man's good is insight into and identification with the One; through some defect—sin, the reducing valve of the conceptual intelligence, etc.—he is exiled from that good. He must in some way overcome the defect and recover the Edenic wholeness which he has lost.

Eckhart's monistic insight was abiding, as was that of Mallarmé. It too lay at the end of the introspective way. In the West the more frequent "way," as we saw earlier, seems to have been that of the extrovertive mystic's transient and gratuitous vision.[4] N. M., looking out over the tenement yard, saw that "everything was *urgent* with life . . . which was the same in the cat, the wasp, the broken bottles, and merely manifested itself differently in these individuals." Huxley understood that "All is in all, —that All is actually which."

Baudelaire speaks of such vision: "C'est une béatitude calme et immobile; tous les problèmes philosophiques sont résolus. Toutes les questions ardues contre lesquelles s'escriment les théologiens, et qui font le désespoir de l'humanité raisonnante, sont limpides et claires. Toute contradiction est devenue unité. L'homme est *passé* Dieu."[5] He is describing a hashish vision, but he points out that drugs are not necessary to produce such states of consciousness. At the end of the article Baudelaire cites "un remarquable philosophe peu connu, Barbereau," to the effect that "moyens artificiels" are unnecessary "pour arriver à la béatitude poétique," since the greatest writers have had the experience without the drug. Adds Baudelaire, "je pense exactement comme lui."[6]

Descriptions of such privileged moments have become quite common in recent western literature. Joyce, in *A Portrait of the Artist as a Young Man*, calls them *epiphanies*. Epiphanies are moments "when the meaningless flow of ideas and perceptions—the 'stream of consciousness'—suddenly makes a kind of sense." In art, the epiphanies give a fourth dimension to what would otherwise remain three-dimensional works, raising them from a conceptual to an ontological level. They are "crossroads in space-time when everything is seen as connected."[7] They are moments when from the psychic swarm of our experience a new *Gestalt* emerges which opens onto cosmic vistas.

Let us take two examples which come to mind almost at random. The first is the poem *Son de cloche* of Pierre Reverdy:

> Tout s'est éteint
> Le vent passe en chantant
> Et les arbres frisonnent
> Les animaux sont morts
> Il n'y a plus personne
> > Regarde
> Les étoiles ont cessé de briller
> > La terre ne tourne plus
> Une tête s'est inclinée
> > Les cheveux balayant la nuit
> Le dernier clocher resté debout
> Sonne minuit

What is the real subject of this poem? The darkness, the silence, the motionlessness of being. Animals are dead, the earth no longer turns. At that moment when it is no longer one day nor yet the next, time is swallowed up into eternity.

A very different kind of passage comes from *Light in August.* Faulkner is talking about the sawmill where Lena's brother is supposed to be working. This leads him into a vision of the abandoned mills of the same type which used to dot the southern woods:

> The brother worked in the mill. All the men in the village worked in the mill or for it. It was cutting pine. It had been there seven years and in seven years more it would destroy all the timber within its reach. Then some of the machinery and most of the men who ran it and existed because of and for it would be loaded onto freight cars and moved away. But some of the machinery would be left, since new pieces could always be bought on the installment plan—gaunt, staring, motionless wheels rising from mounds of brick rubble and ragged weeds with a quality profoundly astonishing, and gutted boilers lifting their rusting and unsmoking stacks with an air stubborn, baffled and bemused upon a stumppocked scene of profound and peaceful desolation, unplowed, untilled, gutting slowly into red and choked ravines beneath the long quiet rains of autumn and the galloping fury of the vernal equinoxes.[8]

The narrative progresses normally enough, when suddenly—for the narrator and for the reader—the experience takes on a "profoundly astonishing" aspect. Both are caught up in the rush of the seasons themselves, and in the desolation and emptiness of being which underlie them.

Examples like these could be multiplied almost indefinitely. Doubtless the reader has some of his own in mind, some of which he might consider more typical than those given here. Proust's whole novel, for example, was built on the epiphanies in his experience.

Mallarmé had such experiences and recreates them in his poetry, but his monistic insight did not derive from them, nor was it limited to them. His vision was not transient but, as we said of Meister Eckhart's, "abiding," the fruit of his long spiritual struggle during the 1860s.

When Mallarmé talked about his monism or wrote of it in letters and articles, he usually expressed himself in literary terms. Best known is this passage from the famous autobiographical letter written to Verlaine in 1885:

> . . . j'ai toujours rêvé et tenté autre chose, avec une patience d'alchimiste, prêt à y sacrifier toute vanité et toute satisfaction, comme on brûlait jadis son mobilier et les poutres de son toit, pour alimenter le fourneau du Grand Oeuvre. Quoi? C'est difficile à dire: un livre, tout bonnement, en maints tomes, un livre qui soit un livre, architectural et prémédité, et non un recueil des inspirations de hasard fussent-elles merveilleuses . . . J'irai plus loin, je dirai: le Livre, persuadé qu'au fond il n'y en a qu'un tenté à son insu par quiconque a écrit, même les génies. L'explication orphique de la terre, qui est le seul devoir du poète et le jeu littéraire par excellence. . . .[9]

The job of the poet, the one who undertakes the "explication orphique de la terre," is to produce the Great Work, the single, unique *Book*. There is only one book, because the reality of the world is not plural but unitary. The driving force of the poet, as Mallarmé conceives him, is the irresistible urge to achieve the "texte véridique": "Plus ou moins, tous les livres, contiennent la fusion de quelques redites comptées: même il n'en serait qu'un—au monde, sa loi—bible comme la simulent les nations. La différence d'un ouvrage à l'autre, offrant autant de leçons proposées dans un immense concours pour le texte véridique."[10]

The "true text" would in some mysterious way recreate the truth of being, which is one truth, eternal, unchanging. It would be the exact symbol of the absolute. An observation of Yeats on "all art that is not mere story-telling" is very close to Mallarmé's meaning here. Yeats says that all such art "is symbolic, and has the purpose of those symbolic talismans which medieval magicians made with complex colors and forms, and bade their patients ponder over daily, and guard with holy secrecy; *for it entangles, in complex colors and forms, a part of the Divine Essence.*"[11]

The italics are mine and point up, at least for the present purpose, the most relevant part of Yeats's remark. For

Mallarmé, the Great Work, if ever achieved, would not "entangle" just a part of the Divine Essence, but the whole of it. No alchemist ever achieved the Great Work, and Mallarmé knows that he probably never will either. Still, even though his goal be out of reach, he will attempt it, hoping to prove "par les portions faites que ce livre existe, et que j'ai connu ce que je n'aurai pas pu accomplir."[12] Perfect coincidence of the work produced and the absolute onto which it is meant to open would be, in the words of the *Faune,* the

> Trop d'hymen souhaité de qui cherche le *la.*

The "perfect cry" and the "constant harmony" of which a poet like Hart Crane speaks, for instance, are never more than imperfectly uttered. Yet even in their imperfections they are supreme achievements of art, they constitute the "jeu littéraire par excellence," the "explication orphique de la terre."[13]

The poem, then, is a part of the all-inclusive *Book,* or Great Work. It is "L'hymne, harmonie et joie, comme pur ensemble groupé dans quelque circonstance fulgurante, des relations entre tout."[14] It is, in itself, an epiphany. The poet does not create new matter to work upon. Materially speaking, his world is the same as ours. What is different is his vision, which, riveted to the plane of Being, sees not the separateness but the unity—the rapports—of all things: "Les choses existent. Nous n'avons pas à les créer. Nous n'avons qu'à en saisir les rapports; et ce sont ces rapports qui forment les vers. . . ."[15] The poet's vision, looking through the many to the One, draws diverse impressions together, overcomes the schisms and contradiction of ordinary thought, and *simplifies the world.* "La nature a lieu," says Mallarmé, "on n'y ajoutera pas. . . . Tout l'acte disponible reste de saisir les rapports, entre temps, rares ou multiples; d'après quelque état intérieur et que l'on veuille à son gré étendre, simplifier le monde."[16]

Guy Michaud sees Mallarmé's insistence on seizing and reproducing the interrelatedness of all things as one of the fundamental principles of his poetic art. Every poem, every word, every image, says Michaud, is for Mallarmé "un point de rencontre," a "carrefour en liaison essentielle avec tout le reste du monde."[17]

The *Verbe* is absolute, infinite. On the human level only particular languages exist, each of which is "le développement du Verbe, son idée dans l'Être, le temps devenu son mode."[18] When a poem succeeds, as Michaud said, in becoming a kind of essential crossroad, it then in its entirety becomes a *new* word, outside and above any known language; it becomes an incantatory power which moves us a step back toward the purity of the *Verbe*. It constitutes, in Mallarmé's words, "un mot total, neuf, étranger à la langue et comme incantatoire."[19] It is more than the sum of its parts: it is a symbol which entangles the divine essence.

In one sense the poem serves the same symbolical function as the "protective circle, the mandala," which, as Jung says, is "the traditional antidote for chaotic states of mind."[20] It discovers the "preexistent meaning in the chaos of life,"[21] and draws form from chaos, unity from diversity.

But the poem is not only an image of order. It is also a *method*—one might almost say a *device*—for attaining vision into the absolute heart of that order. The poem is not only *mandala*, it is also *yantra*. The yantra, etymologically an "instrument for giving the mind control," is an image or geometric design used in certain systems of yoga to aid the mind in its movement out of time and space and into the absolute.[22] In our context we may say that any poem which "entangles the divine" or constitutes a "mot total, neuf . . . incantatoire," performs the same service that the yoga requires and expects of the yantra.

The yantric function of the poem exists on a non-discursive level. It emerges quite mysteriously from the sounds, rhythms, images which together make the whole work. On a discursive level, a poem may make statements *about* the absolute; on the yantric level, which, mistaken for *statement about*, may even seem nonsensical, it opens a way *into* the absolute. We may recall that in his letter to Villiers de l'Isle-Adam (September 1874), Mallarmé said that he reached his knowledge of nothingness by "Sensibilité" alone, not by rational analysis. The success of a poem as yantra is felt rather than understood, which is why Valéry sensed the power of Mallarmé's work before he fully understood its "meaning." The *real* meaning was precisely what he had at first felt. The meaning of a yantric poem is one that the poet or the reader "recognizes by sensation." When Gérard de Nerval warned that attempts at explication would spoil rather than enhance the pleasure to be gotten from his sonnets, he meant what he was saying. His poem was intended as yantra. Explication too often results not so much in elucidation as in reduction of poetry from a yantric to a purely discursive level.

The concept of the yantra throws considerable light on discussions of the problem of defining both "pure" poetry and "poetic" knowledge. The pure poem is the one that exists solely on the yantric level. Its only commerce is with the absolute. The short lyrics of Mallarmé which are cited later in this chapter are as good examples as may be found. An intermediate poetic type would combine yantric and discursive functions. Certainly one of the most perfect examples of this type would be Keats's "Ode on a Grecian Urn." The third kind of verse would exist wholly of the discursive level, with most of Pope and all of Boileau as the most obvious examples. Poetic knowledge—as distinguished from all other kinds—would be that gained through the working of the poem as yantra: ineffable, essential, somehow *right*.

II

To make a poem-yantra Mallarmé in his longer works—*Un coup de dés,* for instance—works by analogy. In the short poems which follow, however, he works by capturing in verse the experience, the very sensation of an epiphany in such a way that it will be recreated in the mind of the reader. The simplest objects and actions are apprehended ontologically. *Petit Air I,* for example, goes like this:

Quelconque une solitude
Sans le cygne ni le quai
Mire sa désuétude
Au regard que j'abdiquai

Ici de la gloriole
Haute à ne la pas toucher
Dont maint ciel se bariole
Avec les ors de coucher

Mais langoureusement longe
Comme de blanc linge ôté
Tel fugace oiseau si plonge
Exultatrice à côté

Dans l'onde toi devenue
Ta jubilation nue.

This poem is in a low key. Charles Mauron is right in saying it is almost an "occasional" work, one of those in which Mallarmé "notes a state of mind, a change of humour, a fugitive thought."[23] But when he concludes that it "can only be enjoyed if we take into account the exact conditions" which gave rise to it, he perhaps goes too far. For beneath its occasional character there is the deeper suggestion of an epiphany, a moment of unitary consciousness.

On a literal level Mauron's analysis seems quite just. It is sunset. Mallarmé, with a young woman, has come to the edge of a river in which the woman is going to swim. He has been looking at the sky, and the colors of a sunset. But its very vividness, its "affectation of glory," causes him to turn away. He reflects on the "abandonment, the 'unusedness' of the bank."

"Suddenly," continues Mauron, "two things happen, almost simultaneously. First a bird, apparently a white bird, gets up, flies skimming the surface, 'languidly' glides along the curve of the river ('coasts'), or rather, as the eye follows the bird, the curve of the river appears to follow its flight. . . . Secondly, the bather dives . . . the sudden movement of the diver has startled the bird. But the poet's mind, turning toward metaphor, creates a more curious relation between them. The white gliding flight of the bird, following the curve of the landscape, is like the final action of slipping off the shift which languidly sweeps the curves of a woman's body...."[24]

Mauron does not go beyond this preliminary work of explication. What happens when one does, when one views the poem from the point of view of the mystic's monistic insight? First of all one notes that the English structure of this sonnet—rarely used by Mallarmé or any other French poet—forces a kind of progressive merging of sense and imagery culminating in the final couplet. Here, all points to the image of the girl splashing jubilantly in the water, and the final idea that this water and this girl have become, for an instant at least, one.

Second, even before diving into the river, the girl herself, through the ellipsis of the comparison and the compression of the metaphor, is made one with the bird:

> Mais langoureusement longe
> Comme de blanc linge ôté
> Tel fugace oiseau....

There is the correspondence between the bird's flight, the lines of the woman's body and the course of the river curving between its banks. There is another between the flight of the bird along the surface of the water and the falling of the "blanc linge" which the woman was wearing. In the end, all three come together. The girl dives into the water, and the bird starts up as the water splashes into the air. In this momentary unity of woman, bird, and water, the universal analogy, the cosmic interrelatedness of all things is revealed to the poet, whose state of mind has in an instant changed from boredom to animation suggested by the words *exultatrice* and *jubilation*. The poet has experienced an epiphany.

The monistic insight of *Quelconque une solitude,* however, is not especially characteristic of Mallarmé. It occurs in the daylight, late in the afternoon, and there is a mood of joyousness, movement, and light which one does not usually find in Mallarmé. (*L'Après-midi d'un faune* is the only important exception to this generalization.) Mallarmé's vision usually seems to be nocturnal, quiet, and, most often, static. *Tout Orgueil,* for instance, one of a triptych of sonnets describing the interior of a room, is a still life. The room, for Mallarmé, symbolizes consciousness, so that this inventory of the objects in the room is at the same time an inventory of the objects of consciousness.

> Tout Orgueil fume-t-il du soir,
> Torche dans un branle étouffée
> Sans que l'immortelle bouffée
> Ne puisse à l'abandon surseoir!
>
> La chambre ancienne de l'hoir
> De maint riche mais chu trophée
> Ne serait pas même chauffée
> S'il survenait par le couloir.
>
> Affres du passé nécessaires
> Agrippant comme avec des serres
> Le sépulcre de désaveu,
>
> Sous un marbre lourd qu'elle isole
> Ne s'allume pas d'autre feu
> Que la fulgurante console.

This poem, like the two others which accompanied it *(Surgi de la croupe et du bond, Une dentelle s'abolit),* has been the subject of much controversial exegesis, most of which has been directed toward clarifying problems of syntax and literal interpretation. Whose is this room, and who is the *hoir,* and what is the *trophée?* On these questions, as on other matters of detail, opinions vary considerably.

Taken as a whole, however, the main outline of the sonnet is clear. The room is the poet's physical and spiritual habitation. It is night, it is cold. No fire burns in the fireplace. In the darkness against one wall can be seen the fire's analogue, a console which seems to lift up its marble top and offer it "to our contemplation, exacting from us, by this mute interjection, some finer interpretation."[25] What is the finer interpretation? Obviously the fire suggests life, and the marble slab—cold, without movement—suggests grave stone and death. But on a more abstract level, the fire suggests becoming while the marble suggests the indivisible One—Being. The fire is warm, sensual, but it consumes itself. The marble is cold and remote—one is reminded of Baudelaire's sonnet on Beauty—but it endures. The tension of the sonnet grows out of the play of the absent fire and the console against one another. The console, here—or rather the marble slab it holds aloft, is, in the truest Proustian sense, a hieroglyph.

The death represented by the extinguished fire is that death to the self which, for those who follow the negative way, precedes illumination. The singularly discomforting insight, or illumination, which this sonnet offers is typical of Mallarmé. If the marble top gives form to truth, it is a truth which excludes the warmth of life and human passion. The infinite is impersonal.

There is another sonnet which metaphorically describes the mystic's state of mind at those moments when he has insight into Being. It is the famous sonnet in *yx:*

> Ses purs ongles très haut dédiant leur onyx,
> L'Angoisse, ce minuit, soutient, lampadophore,
> Maint rêve vespéral brûlé par le Phénix
> Que ne recueille pas de cinéraire amphore
>
> Sur les crédences, au salon vide: nul ptyx,
> Aboli bibelot d'inanité sonore,
> (Car le maître est allé puiser des pleurs au Styx
> Avec le seul objet dont le Néant s'honore.)
>
> Mais proche la croisée au nord vacante, un or
> Agonise selon peut-être le décor
> Des licornes ruant du feu contre une nixe,
>
> Elle, défunte nue en le miroir, encor
> Que, dans l'oubli fermé par le cadre, se fixe
> De scintillations sitôt le septuor.

In an earlier chapter we saw Mallarmé's own explanation of this poem in the letter to Henri Cazalis of July 1868:

J'extrais ce sonnet, auquel j'avais une fois songé, d'une étude
sur la parole: il est inverse, je veux dire que le sens, s'il en a un
(mais je me consolerais du contraire grâce à la dose de poésie
qu'il renferme, ce me semble) est évoqué par un mirage interne
des mots mêmes. En se laissant aller à le murmurer plusiers fois
on éprouve une sensation assez cabalistique . . . il me semble se
prêter à une eau-forte pleine de rêve et de vide.

Par exemple une fenêtre nocturne ouverte, les deux volets
attachés: une chambre avec une personne dedans, malgré l'air
stable que présentent les deux volets attachés, et dans une nuit
faite d'absence et d'interrogation, sans meuble, sinon l'ébauche
plausible de vagues consoles, un cadre belliqueux et agonisant,
du miroir appendu au fond, avec sa reflexion stellaire et incom-
préhensible, de la grande Ourse, qui relie au ciel seul ce logis
abandonné du monde.[26]

Mallarmé's own clarification makes this sonnet easier for
us now, keeping us from the kind of error which, in 1926,
led Camille Mauclair, who did not know the correspondence,
to conclude that it was "le sonnet de l'amour satisfait."[27]
The theme is not one of love. Rather it is that of the apprehension of the absolute in a moment of hermetic identification of microcosm and macrocosm.

That the occult flavor was intentional, Mallarmé shows
by his reference to the Cabala. He also shows that he was
quite consciously writing poems whose sound might work
like an incantation and be more illuminating than their
sense. The "sonorité des mots" will serve a yantric function.

As elsewhere in Mallarmé the room here symbolizes consciousness and the objects—concerns, ambitions, ideas—
which it contains. It represents the time-space world in
which the mind, by its very nature, lives. However, this room
is not wholly enclosed: a window opens out into the night
sky and the stars, representing the possibility of transcendence.

The mirror is special among the objects in the room. It
represents the very core of consciousness, the indivisible
"I-Am" reality of the individual being. This mirror is mute,
utterly passive receptivity. It reflects within its own depths
that which is offered to it—in this case the seven stars of the
Great Bear.

The role of this constellation is most important. We know that Mallarmé spoke of the "danse idéale" of the constellations and that in *Un coup de dés* the constellation seems to represent a pattern of suggested order at the very limit of human consciousness, as far back toward the absolute as the mind of man can go. For the moment it is most important to note that the seven stars of the Great Bear circle eternally around the fixed polar star in the same way that the mystic's gaze remains fixed on the central, unutterable truth of his vision. The north star—fixed, unmoving—has the same function in this sonnet as the "primal point" in mythology or in the speculations of the Cabala. That is, it is the first manifestation in time and space of the Godhead (the Absolute, the Divine), the umbilical point which attaches the manifested world to its ineffable source. It is "the point out of which the world started, spreading itself to right and left and into all directions, and by which it is sustained."[28]

The sense of the sonnet now becomes clear. The room is symbolical of the poet's consciousness. Within it he has been engaged in spiritual work, but with no success. He plunges deeper and deeper into his own being until at the moment of midnight he has reached the Styx and that mystic death to himself which is the condition of revelation. Now only the mirror—the most interior, secret part of the psyche—stands out in the darkness of the room. The mirror is pure openness to Being. All else has fallen away as it stands, silent, motionless, facing the open window. In it is reflected the image of the macrocosmic order itself, the constellation of the Great Bear straining toward the umbilical polar star. In this instant the finite and the infinite, the mirror and the heavens, the poet and the universe, have become *One*.

Notes

1. John Senior, *The Way Down and Out: The Occult in Symbolist Literature* (Ithaca, 1959), p. 39.

2. Quoted in D. T. Suzuki, *Mysticism, Christian and Buddhist* (New York, 1957), p. 7.

3. Quoted in Suzuki, p. 9.

4. Suzuki points out that the introspective way is "natural" to the eastern mystic, but that in the West it is the exception.

5. *Œuvres complètes* (Paris, 1951), pp. 419–420.

6. *Ibid.,* p. 423.

7. Senior, *The Way Down and Out,* pp. xii, xiii.

8. William Faulkner, *Light in August* (New York, 1950), p. 4.

9. *Œuvres complètes,* pp. 622–623.

10. *Ibid.,* p. 367.

11. Quoted in Senior, *The Way Down and Out,* p. 158.

12. *Œuvres,* p. 663.

13. See Hart Crane's "Legend."

14. Mallarmé, *Œuvres,* p. 378.

15. *Ibid.,* p. 871.

16. *Ibid.,* p. 647.

17. *Mallarmé,* p. 59.

18. *Œuvres,* p. 364.

19. *Ibid.,* p. 368.

20. *Works,* IX, 10.

21. *Ibid.,* p. 35.

22. *The Way Down and Out,* p. 18.

23. *Psychanalyse,* p. 158.

24. *Ibid.,* pp. 158–160.

25. *Ibid.,* p. 250.

26. *Propos,* pp. 83–84.

27. Mallarmé, *Œuvres,* p. 1491.

28. *Zohar,* trans. M. Simon (Bennet Publications, n.p., n.d.).

Hierosgamos: Hérodiade
and L'Après-midi d'un faune

Chapter Six

"It was natural and inevitable," says Evelyn Underhill, "that the imagery of human love and marriage should have seemed to the mystic the best of all images of his 'fulfillment of life'. . . . It lay ready to his hand; it was understood by all men; and moreover, it certainly does offer, upon lower levels, a strangely exact parallel to the sequence of states in which man's spiritual consciousness unfolds itself, and which form the consummation of the mystic life."[1] It is the "common opinion," she continues, "that this part of the symbolical vocabulary of the western mystic is "traceable to the popularity of the Song of Songs, regarded as an allegory of the spiritual life." Her own belief, however, lay "rather in the opposite statement: namely, that the mystic loved the Song of Songs because he there saw reflected, as in a mirror, the most secret experiences of his soul: the sense of a desire that was so real, inward and intense that it could be compared with the closest link of human love, of an intercourse that was no mere spiritual self-indulgence but was rooted in the primal duties and necessities of life—more, those deepest, most intimate secrets of communion, those self-giving ecstasies which all mystics know, but of which we, who are not mystics, may not speak—all these he found symbolized and suggested . . . in the poetry which man has invented to honor that passion in which the merely human draws nearest to the divine."[2]

Miss Underhill is surely right. One does not read very far in the mystics without coming upon a great many samples of this kind of *conjunctio* symbolism.[3] Among those from whom we have been quoting, for instance, St. John of the Cross speaks of the soul as being "united with its Beloved in a union of simplicity, purity, faith and similitude."[4] At the end of the soul's spiritual journey, he says, "the Spouse shall take it into the cellar of wine of his perfect love."[5]

For Eckhart the mystical experience is one in which God "begets his son in the core of the soul. There is no other way."[6] St. Bernard, commenting on the line "Let him kiss me with the kisses of his mouth" from the Song of Songs, says that "of all the sentiments of nature, this of love is the most excellent, especially when it is rendered back to him who is the fountain and principle of it—that is, God. Nor are there any expressions equally sweet to signify the mutual affection between the Word of God and the soul, as those of Bridegroom and Bride, inasmuch as between individuals who stand in such relation to each other all things are in common, and they possess nothing separate or divided. They have one inheritance, one dwelling-place, one table, and they are, in fact, one flesh. If, then, mutual love is especially befitting to a bride and bridegroom, it is not unfitting that the name of Bride is given to a soul which loves."[7]

Thomas Aquinas uses the same symbolism: "The soul . . . holds and is herself held; she clasps and she is closely embraced, and by the bond of love she unites herself with God. . . ."[8] And, finally, here is a quotation from the verse of an anonymous Persian mystic:

> Soul becomes pregnant by the Soul of Souls
> And brings forth Christ;
> Not that Christ that walks on land and sea,
> But that Christ that is above space.[9]

There is no need to continue this random sampling. Everyone is familiar, if not with these, at least with similar expressions. The symbolism of the *hierosgamos*—of physical union with the divine—touches on the most central experiences of the mystic: the deep longing of consciousness for reintegration into Being.

The examples we have seen were all in a Christian context. Can they apply to the experience of a non-Christian like Mallarmé? Doubtless they can. The experience itself (as distinct from its interpretation) seems to be fundamentally the same among Christians and Non-Christians alike; the differences which exist between the two groups grow out of the problem of interpretation in secular rather than theological terms. If, in the passages above, one reads illumination for Christ and Absolute for God, he will already be very close to Mallarmé.

Significantly, both of the poems in which this theme is dominant were begun during the years of spiritual crisis. *Hérodiade* and *L'Après-midi d'un faune* are very different poems in atmosphere and expression and yet, when they are viewed from the perspective of the *hierosgamos* they can clearly be seen to treat the same problem, that of the mystic *conjunctio*. Still, there is an important difference here from the examples we have so far reviewed: neither of these poems portrays a fulfillment. Both deal with a union that does not take place. For the poet who is also a mystic, fulfillment requires two unions rather than one: the first is that of the artist-mystic with his absolute, and the second is that of his mystical vision with the "material work to be made," the poem.

II

In a sense *Hérodiade* is Mallarmé's *Faust*. He worked on it for most of his life. We know from the already-quoted letter of October 1864 to Henri Cazalis that he was beginning at that time the elaboration of "ma tragédie d'Hérodiade." And we also know that the manuscript was open on his work table at the time of his death in 1898. First conceived as a tragedy suitable for stage presentation, his theme gradually condensed itself and refined itself into the three fragments

we have today. These—"Ancienne ouverture d'Hérodiade,"
"Scène," and "Cantique de St. Jean"—are best read as separate poems dealing with a common theme. Of these three
only "Scène" was published during Mallarmé's lifetime (in
his collected *Poésies,* in 1887). It is the best known of the
three pieces, and it is the one most relevant to our purpose
here.

The year 1864 marks the threshold of Mallarmé's psychological dark night and, according to his correspondence, it
was his work on *Hérodiade* which led him into it. At that
time he was beginning to experience new insights and feel
new powers within himself and was groping for the poetic that
would express them. Yet, as he began to work, he felt not
exhilaration, but terror; he tells Cazalis that he has finally
begun work on Hérodiade, but "avec terreur, car j'invente
une langue qui doit jaillir d'une poétique très nouvelle.
. . ."[10] The task proved more difficult and more exhausting
than he could ever have imagined. The idea of this poem
obsessed him during the next five years and, except for the
time he spent on the *Faune* and on a small number of sonnets, he worked on it alone. In 1869 a version of the "Scène"
was sent to Catulle Mendès for the first *Parnasse contempo-
rain,* but did not appear. Even after he had submitted it for
publication Mallarmé could not rid himself of his obsessive
subject. A definitive version of the "Scène" was published
only posthumously, along with the companion pieces. He
never really considered it finished.

The poem, which runs to some one hundred and thirty
lines, is too long to reproduce here in its entirety, but we
must have before our eyes certain key passages and fix in our
minds some idea of its general structure. There are but two
characters, an old nurse and the princess, Hérodiade. The
nurse speaks:

> Tu vis! ou vois-je ici l'ombre d'une princesse?
> A mes lèvres tes doigts et leurs bagues. . . .

Hérodiade, however, orders her back. She can permit no touch,
no familiarity:

> Reculez.
> Le blond torrent de mes cheveux immaculés
> Quand il baigne mon corps solitaire le glace
> D'horreur, et mes cheveux que la lumière enlace
> Sont immortels. O femme, un baiser me tûrait
> Si la beauté n'était la mort. . . .

She asks the nurse to hold the mirror for her while she combs her hair. The old woman suggests some perfume. Again she is refused:

> Laisse là ces parfums! ne sais-tu
> Que je les hais, nourrice, et veux-tu que je sente
> Leur ivresse noyer ma tête languissante?

There follows an apostrophe to the mirror, and then the nurse's third "crime," an attempt to rearrange a lock of Hérodiade's hair which has fallen out of place.

> Assez! Tiens devant moi ce miroir.
>   O miroir!
> Eau froide par l'ennui dans ton cadre gelée
> Que de fois et pendant des heures, désolée
> Des songes et cherchant mes souvenirs qui sont
> Comme des feuilles sous ta glace au trou profond,
> Je m'apparus en toi comme une ombre lointaine,
> Mais, horreur! des soirs, dans ta sévère fontaine,
> J'ai de mon rêve épars connu la nudité!
> Nourrice, suis-je belle?
> H.   Un astre, en vérité
> Mais cette tresse tombe. . . .
> N.   Arrête dans ton crime
> Qui refroidit mon sang vers sa source, et réprime
> Ce geste, impiété fameuse. . . .

The triple impiety of the nurse has awakened in Hérodiade a sense of foreboding. The nurse, who notices this and other aberrations of her mistress' behavior, questions her unnatural purity:

> N. Temps bizarre, en effet, de quoi le ciel vous garde!
> Vous errez, ombre seule, et nouvelle fureur,

Et regardant en vous précoce avec terreur;
. . . . et pour qui, dévorée
D'angoisses, gardez-vous la splendeur ignorée
Et le mystère vain de votre être?

H.   Pour moi.

N.   Triste fleur qui croît seule et n'a pas d'autre émoi
Que son ombre dans l'eau vue avec atonie.

H.   . . . . Je ne veux rien d'humain.

Hérodiade continues with a long hymn on her solitude:

H.   Oui, c'est pour moi, pour moi, que je fleuris, déserte!
. . . .
. . . J'aime l'horreur d'être vierge et je veux
Vivre parmi l'effroi que me font mes cheveux
Pour, le soir, retirée en ma couche, reptile
Inviolé sentir en la chair inutile
Le froid scintillement de ta pâle clarté
Toi qui te meurs, toi qui brûles de chasteté,
Nuit blanche de glaçons et de neige cruelle!
Et ta soeur solitaire, ô ma soeur éternelle
Mon rêve montera vers toi: telle déjà
Rare limpidité d'un coeur qui le songea,
Je me crois seule en ma monotone patrie
Et tout, autour de moi, vit dans l'idolâtrie
D'un miroir qui reflète en son calme dormant
Hérodiade au clair regard de diamant . . .
O charme dernier, oui! je le sens, je suis seule.

The nurse does not understand; she is afraid her mistress
may be dying. Hérodiade calms and dismisses her, but not
before having asked her to close the blinds:

L'azur
Séraphique sourit dans les vitres profonds,
Et je déteste, moi, le bel azur!

She imagines some possible escape, perhaps to

. . . un pays
Où le sinistre ciel ait les regards haïs
De Vénus qui, le soir, brûle dans le feuillage;
J'y partirais.

But in the concluding speech she rejects such flight:

> H.   Vous mentez, ô fleur nue
> De mes lèvres.
>   J'attends une chose inconnue
> Ou peut-être, ignorant le mystère et vos cris,
> Jetez-vous les sanglots suprêmes et meurtris
> D'une enfance sentant parmi les rêveries
> Se séparer enfin ses froides pierreries.

The subject, as Mallarmé develops it, owes nothing more than its name to biblical sources. For his part Henri Mondor suggested that Mallarmé's Hérodiade may be "un écho de la Salammbô de Flaubert,"[11] which had appeared some eighteen months earlier. Albert Thibaudet believed that the character of the heroine may have been suggested by the sonnet of Baudelaire which ends:

> Ses yeux sont faits de minéraux charmants
> Et dans cette nature étrange et symbolique
> Où l'ange inviolé se mêle au sphynx antique,
>
> Où tout n'est qu'or, acier, lumière et diamants
> Resplendit à jamais comme un astre inutile
> La froide majesté de la femme stérile.[12]

There are obvious similarities between these lines and some of those in which Mallarmé describes the appearance and mental state of Hérodiade. But it would be a mistake to see in Mallarme's poem nothing more than the "froide majesté de la femme stérile." If she is sterile, her sterility is of a very special kind.

It seems most likely that when he undertook this work, Mallarmé had no sense of what it would become. He conceived it as a drama, and seriously hoped to see it played, perhaps at the Théâtre Français, where, as Théodore de Banville wrote him, he would find "justement ce qu'il faut comme décor pour le monter. . . ." But the very writing of the poem seemed to reveal to him its higher purpose and its most intimate relation to his own state of mind. It ended by drawing him deep down within himself, into the darkest night of the very core of the soul, where, as Eckhart says, "one discovers the central silence . . . where no creature may enter, nor any idea, and there the soul neither thinks nor acts, nor entertains any idea, either of itself or of anything else."[13] He was drawn into nothingness. In her coldness and in her rejection of all contact with the finite and the living, and in her sense of foreboding, Hérodiade mirrors the conditions and the terror of this confrontation of consciousness with the dark horizon of its existence.

Eckhart says, "God and I, we are one."[14] Outside the Christian context the mystic says, "The Absolute and I, we are one." And the mode of knowledge of this absolute, at least for those mystics like Mallarmé, is the way of introspection. This accounts for the so-called narcissism of Hérodiade. Narcissism is of course present, but its significance is transcendental. Merely to name it is not to say much about it. Hérodiade, looking into her mirror, is probing her own consciousness for an answer to the mystery of life. Sometimes she seems almost to have grasped it, to have reached the core of emptiness, and to have been terrified. She has known, she says, the "nudité" of her "rêve épars." The mirror here, as in the sonnet in *yx,* symbolizes human consciousness turned toward the absolute within, awaiting an absolute reflection.

If Hérodiade is narcissistic and solitary, if she retreats before the threat of contact with the merely human, it is because she is awaiting the "chose inconnue," a kind of parthenogenesis of the spirit which will at the same time fertilize her and keep her pure for the work to be done. But the movement of the poem is never completed, the fertilizing union never takes place. The mirror reflects her gaze back upon itself.

The union Hérodiade admittedly awaits at the end of the poem might have produced the work that Mallarmé was not able to write. But it might also have destroyed the possibility of writing it. Hérodiade has glimpsed the way, but cannot let herself go. What paradox holds her back? Narcissus, attracted too much to his own image, drowned himself in it. His beauty was his death. Hérodiade, too, knows that beauty is death:

> Un baiser me tûrait / Si la beauté n'était la mort.

This relationship of beauty and death is the key to a complete understanding of this poem, and to an understanding of a most important part of Mallarmé's thought in general: the so-called problem of sterility.

III

"Dans l'oeuvre de Stéphane Mallarmé," says Albert Thibaudet, "*L'Après-midi d'un faune* est la pièce des connaisseurs." Why? Because, Thibaudet suggests, of the absolute fusion of style, symbol, and subject: "Mallarmé, au fur et à mesure de la composition poétique, laisse spontanément, sans intention artificielle et sans concordance forcée, se déposer, dans les lignes du sujet érotique, des symboles que, moitié de nous-mêmes et moitié des allusions indiquées, nous menons jusqu'à un ciel métaphysique et calme."[15] In the light of later criticism (Thibaudet wrote in the second decade of this century) this poem has been somewhat displaced from the central position it had for Thibaudet. But if it is read carefully, along with *Hérodiade* especially, no one can doubt that it does lead into one very important sector of that "ciel métaphysique" whose translation into art was Mallarmé's single goal.

After the first bitter and exhausting winter of work on *Hérodiade,* Mallarmé put it aside for his new work: "J'ai laissé Hérodiade pour les cruels hivers: cette oeuvre solitaire m'avait stérilisé et, dans l'intervalle, je rime un intermède héroïque dont le héros est un Faune. Ce poème renferme une très haute et très belle idée. Mais les vers sont terriblement difficiles à faire, car je la fais scénique, non possible au théâtre mais exigeant le théâtre. Et cependant je veux conserver toute la poésie de mes oeuvres lyriques. . . . J'ajoute que je compte la présenter en août au Théâtre Français."

In atmosphere the *Faune* will be everything that *Hérodiade* is not: diurnal, flooded with light and open to the air of summer, mediterranean and pastoral in mood. Yet its subject is, as we shall see, nearly identical to that of its nocturnal sister.

The work of composition remained as difficult as ever. "Tu ne saurais croire comme il est difficile de s'acharner au vers que je veux très neuf et très beau. . . . Mais si tu savais que de nuits désespérées et de jours de rêverie il faut sacrifier avant de faire des vers originaux (ce que je n'ai jamais fait jusqu'ici) et digne dans leurs suprêmes mystères, de rejouir l'âme d'un poète.[16] When the first version of his poem, which he called *Monologue d'un faune,* was not found suitable for stage presentation, he continued to work on it, passing through a second stage—*Improvisation d'un faune*—to the final version, which was not completed until 1875. Again, as with *Hérodiade,* he seems to have become fully aware of the possibilities of his poem only as he was writing it. It was finally published in 1876, in a deluxe edition, with illustrations by Manet.

The theme is quite simple. A faun (satyr) is awakened near noon on a hot summer's day. His senses are dulled by sleep and the stifling heat, but he knows that he has either dreamed of two nymphs, or has in reality held them before falling asleep. The faun's monologue is his attempt to recapture for himself the reality of his vision—if that is what it was—and to "perpetuate" it. In other words, the theme is that of the artist and of the vision which he must "entangle" in his art:

> Ces nymphes, je les veux perpétuer.
> Si clair,
> Leur incarnat léger, qu'il voltige dans l'air
> Assoupi de sommeils touffus.
> Aimai-je un rêve?

The faun tries to remember:

> *"Que je coupais ici les creux roseaux domptés*
> *Par le talent; quand, sur l'or glauque de lointaines*

> *Verdures dédiant leur vigne à des fontaines,*
> *Ondoie une blancheur animale au repos:*
> *Et qu'au prélude lent où naissent les pipeaux*
> *Ce vol de cygnes, non! de naïades se sauve*
> *Ou plonge. . . ."*

The symbolism here is autonomous, yet beautifully transparent. The faun cuts a reed, the instrument of his art. The reed, of course, may itself at one time have been a nymph. At the first notes of his reed-flute, there starts up in the distance a white form, "une blancheur animale." Is it perhaps a swan? No, those are naiads which are diving into the river, or running away into the woods.

Yet all this has disappeared now without a trace:

> Inerte, tout brûle dans l'heure fauve
> Sans marquer par quel art ensemble détala
> Trop d'hymen souhaité de qui cherche le *la:*

The point of the *la* is an important one. Delfel sees in it only a way of saying that the faun is trying out his flute.[17] But the *la,* A, is the tuning note, the pitch against which all others are measured, the absolute pitch. To achieve that absolute pitch is the "trop d'hymen" for which the faun wishes and also that desired by the poet who aims for the perfect work.

The faun discovers one sign, however, that his adventure was real:

> Mon sein, vierge de preuve, atteste une morsure
> Mystérieuse, due à quelque auguste dent. . . .

Perhaps he can recapture his vision through the music of his flute:

> Tâche donc, instrument des fuites, ô maligne
> Syrinx, de refleurir aux lacs où tu m'attends!
> Moi, de ma rumeur fier, je vais parler longtemps
> De déesses; et par d'idolâtres peintures,
> A leur ombre enlever encore des ceintures:
> Ainsi quand des raisins j'ai sucé la clarté,
> Pour bannir un regret par ma feinte écarté,

Rieur, j'élève au ciel d'été la grappe vide
Et, soufflant dans ses peaux lumineuses, avide
D'ivresse, jusqu'au soir je regarde au travers.

The "idolâtres peintures" can be understood as works of art, at least once removed from the reality they pretend to represent. It is through them that the faun seeks out the truth of his dream. Here, of course, the art in question is music, but the thought is generalized through the lines on the grape-intoxication-inspiration through which, after having "sucé la clarté" from within them, he will then look at the world.

And, in fact, he does come a step closer to remembering exactly what took place:

"*Mon oeil, trouant les joncs, dardait chaque encolure*
Immortelle, qui noie dans l'onde sa brûlure
Avec un cri de rage au ciel de la forêt;
Et le splendide bain de cheveux disparaît
Dans les clartés et les frissons, ô pierreries!
J'accours; quand, à mes pieds, s'entrejoignent (meurtries
De la langueur goûtée á ce mal d'être deux)
Des dormeuses parmi leurs seuls bras hasardeux;
Je les ravis, sans les désenlacer, et vole
A ce massif, haï par l'ombrage frivole,
De roses tarissant tout parfum au soleil,
Où notre ébat au jour consumé soit pareil."

The faun, investigating the naiads, finds that all have fled except two whom he finds asleep in each other's arms, and whom he takes away with him. But he will not be successful in the fulfillment of his desire:

"*Mon crime, c'est d'avoir, gai de vaincre ces peurs*
Traîtresses, divisé la touffe échevelée
De baisers que les dieux gardaient si bien mêlée,
Car, à peine j'allais cacher un rire ardent
Sous les replis heureux d'une seule ...
Que de mes bras, défaits par de vagues trépas,
Cette proie, à jamais ingrate se délivre
Sans pitié du sanglot dont j'étais encore ivre."

"Et voilà," says Mme Soula, "la fin de l'aventure sentimentale. Le Faune a vu s'évanouir les nymphes sous ses

baisers au moment où il allait joyeusement les posséder."[18]
The faun has dreamed a union which, like that of
Hérodiade, remains unconsummated. But if conscious means
cannot lead him back to the nymph he so desires, he will
again try unconscious ones. He will give up the poem for the
poetic experience itself:

> Non, mais l'âme
> De paroles vacante et ce corps alourdi
> Tard succombent au fier silence de midi:
> Sans plus il faut dormir en l'oubli du blasphème,
> Sur le sable altéré gisant et comme j'aime
> Ouvrir ma bouche à l'astre éfficace des vins!
>
> Couple, adieu; je vais voir l'ombre que tu devins.

That is, he is going back to sleep. At this point one understands more fully the significance of the title of this poem. The
faun's monologue takes place at noon. The real subject of the
poem is precisely that which no poem can express: the actual
union which may again take place during the dreams of the
faun's afternoon.

IV

It remains now for us to go back and resolve some questions
left unanswered earlier. What indeed is that relationship between beauty and death which Hérodiade knows to be true;
and what is the paradox which stands in the way of her
fulfillment? Why can the faun know his vision only in
dream? Eckhart quoted "one saint" to the effect that "if anyone imagines that he knows God and his knowledge takes
form, then he may know something, but it is not God."[19]
And he continues in his own words: "Three things there are
that hinder one from hearing the eternal Word: The first is
corporeality, the second, number, and the third, time."[20]
Now the mystic's *vision* is above time and outside of space.
So far there is no problem. But if the mystic is also a poet,
he is obsessed with the desire to make his vision into a poem,
and so "body forth the forms of things unknown." Unfortu-

nately the very conditions of a poet's existence are the same categories of corporeality, number, and time which Eckhart warned against. To maintain an extra-temporal and extra-spatial union would involve an abdication of art; to maintain art would be to retreat from union. Or at least it would seem so. The whole poetic quest of Mallarmé was for the method which would maintain both and so combine, as Valéry said, "le simultanée de la vision avec le successif de la parole."[21]

Mallarmé must always have known that he could never wholly succeed. When Hérodiade said that beauty was death, she recognized that to maintain a perfect vision of beauty involved dying to oneself as an artist, that the roles of mystic and maker are irreconcilable in any absolute sense. Even in the purest work there must always remain the barest tincture of failure.

The artist, insofar as he is the creator of works, must always stop short of the point where fulfillment is death. Wallace Fowlie says that in *Hérodiade* Mallarmé left off just on this side of the point where poetry passes into the realm of the unexpressed.[22] This seems to me true not only of *Hérodiade,* but of almost all the verse Mallarmé wrote after 1865. In his "Cantique de St. Jean" Mallarmé is really talking about himself. He tried to remain in his verse as close to his own vision as St. John had been to his martyrdom just before the blade severed his head. But proximity is not union.

The hierosgamos is the mystic's supreme joy. For the poet it can also be the supreme torture. At the same moment that it teaches him the amplitude of being, it also teaches him the limitations of his art. Hérodiade and the faun, in their inability to achieve union, represent this inevitable failure.

Notes

1. *Mysticism*, pp. 136–137.

2. *Ibid.*, p. 137.

3. Jung has discussed *conjunctio* symbolism at length in volume 14 of his collected works.

4. *The Dark Night of the Soul*, p. 30.

5. *Ibid.*, p. 49.

6. Raymond B. Blakney, *Meister Eckhart: A Modern Translation* (New York, 1941), p. 98.

7. Quoted in Underhill, *Mysticism*, p. 138.

8. Quoted in M. A. Ewer, *A Survey of Mystical Symbolism* (London, 1933), p. 168.

9. *Ibid.*, p. 161. The writer is not identified by Ewer.

10. *Propos*, p. 43.

11. *Vie de Mallarmé*, p. 1441.

12. *Poésie de Mallarmé*, p. 31.

13. Blakney, *Eckhart*, p. 36.

14. *Ibid.*, p. 182.

15. *Poésie de Mallarmé*, p. 393.

16. Mallarmé, *Œuvres*, p. 1449.

17. *Pages choisies*, p. 52.

18. Camille Soula, *Gloses sur Mallarmé* (Paris, 1946), p. 275.

19. Blakney, *Eckhart*, p. 219.

20. *Ibid.*, p. 203.

21. Wallace Fowlie, *Mallarmé* (Chicago, 1950), p. 231.

22. *Ibid.*, p. 232.

Chapter Seven | The katabasis, that is, the account of what some trustworthy soul had seen in the world of the dead.
—M. Ewer

Mallarmé also gives form to his mystical experience in terms of the language of spiritual progress, or, more specifically, of the *katabasis*. This is the symbolism of Igitur, the metaphysical shade, who leaves the "room" of finite consciousness, descends the stairway of being to his final mystic death.

The language of spiritual progress—of the allegorical movement of consciousness from one level of being to another—is most often associated with the introvertive kind of experience like that which Mallarmé described in his correspondence. The narrative form of the allegory seems compatible with the longer duration of the inner crisis. Such mystics, says Evelyn Underhill, are acutely aware of "their own imperfection, and of the unutterable perfection of the Absolute life for which they long. . . ." To them their "remaking or regeneration appears . . . as the primal necessity."[1]

In alchemical terms—and let us remember that Mallarmé spoke of the alchemists as "nos ancêtres"—this regeneration requires purification of all baser spiritual elements so that the gold of the illuminated soul may shine through. On the mystical level man himself is the vessel, the *athanor,* in which the alchemical transmutation occurs. The greater part of the vocabulary of esoteric alchemy is devoted to describing the progress of the spirit of man from its state of corruption to that of purity.

73

Although Mallarmé was interested in alchemy and even drew comparisons from its lexicon, he expressed his own spiritual progress in terms of a vocabulary more ancient still, one which in every age has emerged to bear anew a deep truth of human experience: the vocabulary of katabasis, of the descent of the soul into the nether world and death and its subsequent resurrection to a new life. The obvious source for this symbolism is the daily cycle of the rising and setting of the sun, the monthly waxing and waning of the moon, and the yearly alternation of life and death in the succession of the seasons. The earliest peoples at once grasped the significance of these changes. To rise again to new life, one must first go down into death. There are few mythologies or literatures which do not include some version of the katabasis. There are Dionysos, Ishtar, Osiris; there are journeys into the lower worlds of Ulysses and Aeneas; and there is the great symbolism of Dante's *Commedia*.

Symbols of katabasis are not limited to ritualistic or literary use. Jung has found them to be a constant content of the dreams of patients who have reached the threshold of psychic insight, or who are on the verge of psychic crises. One of his patients, a minister, dreamt of himself standing on the crest of a hill, looking down into a valley in which he saw a deep dark pool of water. He *knows*, in his dream, that he must submerge himself in that pool. That will be the price of his achieving psychic balance.[2] The pool, of course, is the unconscious mind, or the underworld, or mystic death. The three are here equivalent; all involve movement away from the ordinary level of life, and down into and through unsounded depths of the soul. By this movement man attains insights which would never have been his had he remained on the more superficial plane. The particular form those insights take depends on the context of the spiritual journey, whether it be Buddhist, aesthetic, psychological, etc. But in spite of varying content, the archetypal katabasis clearly shines through all differences of interpretation. It does so, for instance, in Mallarmé's *Igitur*.

An instance of this archetype very relevant to the autobiographical *conte* of Mallarmé is both mythical and mystical: that of the poet-prophet Orpheus, and the Dionysiac mysteries said to have been founded by him. We recall that in his letter to Verlaine Mallarmé described the poet's mission as nothing less than "l'explication orphique de la terre," that is, as mystical insight poetically expressed. It will be worth while to look at the orphic doctrine a bit more closely.

Orpheus is not mentioned in either Homer or Hesiod. Yet in the sixth century, when we first hear of him, there is already extant a considerable body of poetry attached to his name. Orpheus was said to have descended from Apollo. In the course of his life he made his own journey into hell in an attempt to rescue his beloved Eurydice. This qualified him for the job of guiding others along the same way. Orpheus was finally dismembered by the Maenades, supposedly for having divulged certain secret mysteries to women. His severed head was thrown into the river Hebrus, down which it floated to the sea, all the while uttering oracles and singing. He had been given his lyre by Apollo and instructed in its use by the muses themselves. After his death it became a constellation.

If Orpheus was a prophet of Dionysos, the sect he is said to have founded was a reformed one, having nothing more in common with the older, orgiastic, Dionysian revels than the name of the god they celebrated. Above all else the orphic doctrine was one of detachment from the sensual life, one not at all incompatible with later Christian morality.

The Orphics did not invent new myths; they transformed and infused new meaning into myth already at hand— principally that of Dionysos. According to early accounts Dionysos was given the throne of Olympus in the absence of his father, Zeus. Hera, who was jealous, "then stationed her followers, called Titans, in the inner part of the palace, and with the aid of rattles and a mirror of ingenious workmanship so distracted his childish mind that he left his royal seat and was brought to the place of ambush, led there by the irrational impulse of childhood."[3] Caught by his enemies, Dionysos was killed, then dismembered and devoured. Zeus, however, managed to rescue the heart, from which, according to the most usual account, he caused Dionysos to be reborn. The Titans were reduced to ashes, from which man was then created.

The point of this account, and one which was central to the Orphics, was that of the composite nature of man: evil insofar as he was born of the ashes of the Titans, divinely innocent in that those ashes contained the body of the child-god Dionysos. Initiates recognized the death of Dionysos as that event which, when recapitulated in ritual form, would enable them to slough off the Titanic impurities and realize the Dionysiac potential within them. For the Orphic, as V. D. Macchioro has pointed out, ritual was "a mimetic communion by which the divine nature was attained in real life." It constituted a "starting point for a new life, or for a mystic palingenesis."[4]

Igitur is a narrative which relates the spiritual progress of a latter-day initiate into mystic death and union with the divine. But there are some reservations, some peculiar twists to the story. Obviously, Igitur is Mallarmé himself, who, this one time following out to its conclusion the logic of his vision, passes beyond the penultimate of art to an ultimate and absolute death. "La mort spirituelle du poète," says Guy Michaud, "tel est précisément le sujet d'Igitur."[5]

II

After his spiritual crisis, Mallarmé felt that in order to recover his selfhood—and his vocation as artist—he must gain some perspective, some objective view of what he had been through. One way to accomplish this objectivity, he felt, was to separate himself from his experience by incorporating it into a work of art.

He would make it into a narrative. On the fourteenth of November 1869 he wrote to Henri Cazalis about a new work: "C'est un conte par lequel je veux terrasser le vieux monstre de l'impuissance, son sujet, du reste afin de me cloîtrer dans mon grand oeuvre déjà réétudié. S'il est fait (le conte), je suis guéri; *similia similibus*."[6] Thus, as Guy Michaud points out, Igitur is not a "partie intégrante de l'Œuvre," but a kind of psychological introduction to it, in which Mallarmé tries to describe "son mal pour s'en guérir."[7] The writing of *Igitur* marks Mallarmé's definitive emergence from his personal katabasis, from his dark night of the soul. Having conquered, thanks in part to *Igitur,* the obsessional, debilitating aspect of his experience, "il sent naître en lui l'homme nouveau, il sait . . . que le Livre, le grimoire, le Grand Œuvre . . . doit être désormais sa tâche unique."[8]

Igitur was not published in Mallarmé's lifetime, a fact which attests to the personal nature of the document and the use it was meant to serve. It did not see the light of day until it appeared in a Gallimard edition, with a preface by Dr. Edmond Bonniot, the son-in-law of the poet, who reconstructed the text as we now know it. Dr. Bonniot discovered the work in 1900, when with Geneviève Mallarmé, then his fiancée, he went through a number of Mallarmé's notes and papers which he had found "reserrés dans de grandes boîtes à thé de Chine, en bois."[9] Among them was a notebook, on the cover of which appeared the words

Igitur. Déchet
La folie d'Elbéhnon

Dr. Bonniot had once heard Mallarmé speak of this work, but had never seen the text himself. What he discovered as he read through the notes was not a finished work, but a number of fragments, some in ink, some in pencil, in handwriting "visiblement de différentes époques."[10] The oldest of the fragments were by far the greater in number and also the most finished. The greater part of this work was written between 1867 and 1870, and in August of the latter year Mallarmé is known to have read a version of his *conte* to Catulle Mendès and Villiers de l'Isle-Adam, who had come to visit him in Avignon.

Gardner Davies is of the opinion that the notes for *Igitur* ought to be considered preliminary stages in the composition of *Un coup de dés* rather than bits of a never-completed work. That, he says, is the sense of the word *Déchet* which

Dr. Bonniot saw. Mallarmé elsewhere used this word to designate material left over from a finished work. But even if Davies' view were true, and it is not certain, there would remain such an undeniably important thematic, stylistic, and chronological distance between the two "versions" that *Igitur* must surely be studied separately, in its own right. The same set of ideas is taken up again in *Un coup de dés,* but the whole metaphorical setting is changed and the conclusion is altered.

The main clue to the proper ordering of the notes was provided by a slip of paper on which Mallarmé seems to have outlined his intentions. The narrative will, he indicates, include four "morceaux":

1. Le Minuit
2. L'escalier
3. Le coup de dés
4. Le sommeil sur les cendres, après la bougie soufflée.[11]

Dr. Bonniot arbitrarily adds a fifth section, between the second and third items listed above: "La Vie d'Igitur." This interpolated material is more concrete and deals relatively clearly with the evolution of Igitur's state of mind.

Perhaps it would be worthwhile here to give the text of the "Argument" as Mallarmé wrote it. Although it is the barest outline of what the poet intended to say, it is nevertheless indispensable for grasping the continuity of the whole account, which may be the most obscure writing Mallarmé ever did.

A peu près ce qui suit:

Minuit sonne—le Minuit où doivent être jetés les dés. Igitur descend les escaliers, de l'esprit humain, va au fond des choses: en "absolu" qu'il est. Tombeaux—cendres (pas sentiment, ni esprit) neutralité. Il récite la prédiction et fait le geste. Indifférence. Sifflements dans l'escalier. "Vous avez tort" nulle émotion. L'infini sort du hasard, que vous avez nié. Vous, mathématiciens expirâtes—moi projeté absolu. Devais finir en Infini. Simplement parole et geste. Quant à ce que je vous dis, pour expli-

quer ma vie. Rien ne restera de vous—L'infini enfin échappe de
la famille, qui en a souffert, —vieil espace—pas de hasard. Elle a
eu raison de le nier, —sa vie—pour qu'il ait été absolu. Ceci devait
avoir lieu dans les combinaisons de l'Infini vis-à-vis de l'Absolu.
Nécessaire—extrait l'Idée. Folie utile. Un des actes de l'Univers
vient d'être commis là. Plus rien, restait le souffle, fin de parole
et geste unis—souffle la bougie de l'être par quoi tout a été.
Preuve.

(Creuser tout cela)[12]

In *Igitur* the setting is again a room. The time is midnight, the time when, as Reverdy said, "tout est éteint." It is
the hour when "de l'infini se séparent les constellations et la
mer, demeurées, en l'extériorité, de réciproques néants, pour
en laisser l'essence, à l'heure unie, faire le présent absolu des
choses." The room at midnight is "une chambre du temps
où le mystérieux ameublement arrête un vague frémissement
de pensée, lumineuse brisure du retour des ondes et de leur
élargissement premier, cependant que s'immobilise . . . la
place antérieur de la chute de l'heure en un calme nar-
cotique de *moi* longtemps rêvé." In this night Igitur, an
"antique idée," stirs, he will leave the room of time. He
speaks: "Adieu nuit, que je fus, ton propre sépulcre, mais
qui, l'ombre survivante, se métamorphosera en éternité."

At this point, according to the title given to the next
section, Igitur "quitte la chambre et se perd dans l'escalier."
He then experiences a "vision de la chute interrompue de
panneaux"; he descends in a "spirale vertigineuse." There is
a "fuite indéfinie," and then Igitur—now referred to simply
as "l'Ombre"—finds before him, "en un puits, l'étendu de
couches d'ombre, rendus à la nuit pure, de toutes ses nuits
pareilles apparues, des couches à jamais séparées d'elles et
que sans doute elles ne connurent pas—qui n'est je le sais,
que le prolongement absurde de bruit de la fermeture de la
porte sépulcrale dont l'entrée de ce puits rappelle la porte."

Before this deep well of shadow, Igitur hesitates. Shall he
join the shadows, to become a part of the infinite night? He
hears the beating of his living heart, the timed rhythm of his
humanity. He speaks again: "Je n'aime pas ce bruit. . . .

J'aimerais rentrer dans mon Ombre incréé et antérieur. . . .
He resolves to "dissolve himself into himself."[13] He will not
maintain consciousness, that "seul reste d'ambiguïté," but will
pass beyond it.

However, he must first accomplish the *acte,* the *geste,* the
coup de dés, which will *perhaps* annul time and rescue his
"race" from chance. He knows that this act is a kind of
"folie" and that it is "parfaitement absurde sauf que mouvement (personnel) rendu à l'Infini. . . ." This movement rendered unto the infinite is a purification of the movement—
temporal and spatial—in oneself. Igitur acts, he throws the
dice: ". . . le mouvement qui est en lui est absous."[14] But the
nature and the efficacy of this absolution are left in doubt.

Igitur now accomplishes his destiny. Having acted, he re-
clines on "les cendres des astres"[15] and blows out the candle
of existence. He reenters the dark unity of being.

III

However obscure in detail Mallarmé's narrative is, from the
larger point of view there can be little doubt as to its intent.
Igitur, as Davies said, is motivated by a "désir ancestral
d'abolir le hasard."[16] This chance against which he acts re-
sumes all that characterizes what Plato would call the "realm
of the many." It is the form the world takes for reason, for
analytical intelligence.

And here again one discovers the essential paradox which
the orphic poet must face. Chance can never be finally overcome except by the abolition of consciousness itself. That is
why Igitur goes beyond the *acte* to extinguish the candle of
life itself. Mystic consciousness demands that chance be tran-
scended, but the only means of doing so is to destroy precisely that consciousness which desired the transcendence.
Consciousness itself is the non-absolute in the heart of being;
and chance, number, finitude are its modes of existence. The
work of art, even the most perfect yantric poem, while point-
ing and reaching beyond, still remains caught in the present,

in time. It will never abolish chance. Chance is abolished only at the moment that the mind in which it exists also disappears.

Notes

1. *Mysticism,* p. 140.

2. Jung, *Works,* IX, 34.

3. Qirmicus Maternus, *On the Errors of the Pagan Religions,* quoted in W. C. K. Guthrie, *Orpheus and Greek Religion* (London, 1952), pp. 108–109.

4. *From Orpheus to Paul* (New York, 1930), p. 100.

5. Michaud, *Mallarmé,* p. 78.

6. *Œuvres,* p. 1580.

7. *Mallarmé,* p. 78.

8. *Ibid.,* p. 85.

9. Mallarmé, *Œuvres,* p. 423.

10. *Ibid.,* p. 424.

11. *Ibid.,* p. 434.

12. *Ibid.,* p. 434.

13. *Ibid.,* pp. 435–438 passim.

14. *Ibid.,* p. 442.

15. *Ibid.,* p. 443.

16. *Explication rationelle,* p. 62.

Chapter Eight | *Ne trouvez-vous pas que c'est un acte de démence?*
—Mallarmé

There could be no more apt introduction to this last and most audacious of Mallarmé's works than the following passage from one of the sermons of Meister Eckhart. Describing the soul's movement toward union with the divine, Eckhart writes: ". . . the human spirit takes not its rest. It presses into the vortex, the source in which the spirit originates. There the spirit, in knowing, has no use for number, for numbers are of use only within time, in this defective world. No one can strike his roots into eternity without being rid of the concept of number. The human spirit must go beyond all number-ideas, must break past and away from all ideas of quantity, and then it will be broken into by God."[1] In *Un coup de dés* Mallarmé is writing of absolute knowledge, of the necessity which he feels—and the impossibility in which he finds himself—of transcending in his art the realm of "number-ideas."

Is *Un coup de dés* poem or prose? Mallarmé meant it to be both, and more. Its visual effects alone—the field of the constellations, the "plume solitaire" lost against the vastness of space, the night storm on the primeval waters—raise it out of existing classifications into its own unique category. Readers of the May 1897 issue of the review *Cosmopolis* found some twenty pages given over to the reproduction of what must have seemed to all but a very few subscribers a particularly perverse kind of linguistic madness. Spread across page after page were the dislocated words, phrases, and typographic eccentricities which caused Mallarmé himself, on first showing the proof of his work to the youthful Valéry, to remark: "Ne trouvez-vous pas que c'est un acte de démence?"[2]

A singular feature of this strange work is that, for all its unconventionality of form and obscurity of detail, its purely intellectual content is really clearer than that of any other of Mallarmé's mature poems. On the level of idea it is even rather banal. But the central idea itself, that no human act can abolish the fact of human contingency, shades off into the mystery of the "circonstances éternelles" which surround every idea, and it is precisely into these eternal circumstances that the reader is projected. In *Un coup de dés* Mallarmé's poetic vision achieves the breadth and universality of myth itself. It opens for the reader onto a cosmic, archetypal mime whereby he relives in a moment the whole history of human life and consciousness. He vicariously experiences man's fate.

II

Erich Neumann, in his book on the *Origins and History of Consciousness,* shows how the basic cycle of myth reflects the successive stages in the evolution of consciousness. Basing himself for the most part on Jung's investigations of archetypes, Neumann describes four main stages in the mythic drama: that of the timeless and dimensionless beginning, of the self-devouring serpent, the uroboros; that of the separation of the world parents and the coming of consciousness; that of the affirmation of itself by consciousness as opposed to and distinct from the featureless totality of the unitary womb, but also as frail and menaced by it; and that of the inevitable death of consciousness and return to the primal source.

"The time of the beginning," writes Neumann, "before the coming of the opposites, must be understood as self description of that great epoch when there was still no consciousness. . . . Sun, moon and stars, these symbols of time and therefore of mortality, have not yet been created; day and night, yesterday and tomorrow; genesis and decay, the flux of life and birth and death have not yet entered into the world. This prehistoric state of being is not time, but eternity. . . . And just as there is no time before the birth of man and ego, only eternity, so there is no space, only infinity."[3]

The emerging and epiphenomenal ego first becomes aware of itself as existing over against and separated from this timeless uroboric unity. And it does so at a great price, for the habitation of its awareness is time, finitude and mortality. It feels itself weak and "defenceless against the maelstrom of mysterious being which swamps it again and again."[4]

The loss of wholeness and total unconscious integration with the world, Neumann continues, "is experienced as the primary loss; it is the original deprivation which occurs at the very outset of the ego's evolution."[5] Mankind has become aware of its own existence only by situating itself within the contingent realm of Eckhart's "number ideas." One recalls Coleridge's remark that the creation of consciousness was also the creation of "the non-absolute."

Neumann everywhere stresses the fact that the symbolism of the myths, like that of the "dream and the work of art" is not philosophy or speculation but spontaneous psychic projection. It "rises up" of itself from the depths of the psyche. Neumann is not alone in his treatment of myth, as the work of Eliade, Campbell, and others attest. But in the coherence of his case, and in his close linking of it to the history of consciousness, he is quite original.

III

Symbolically the progression which Neumann describes moves from undifferentiated and featureless void to the separation of the world parents and the consequent creation within the absolute of the "bubble" of time-space where consciousness lives out its adventure. Often this bubble—and the world it contains—is again and again reabsorbed into the nothingness from which it emerged. Hindu lore, for instance, divides history into an endless series of cosmic cycles, each of which includes the birth, life and death of an entire universe.

For the Egyptians the ur-reality was that of the primeval waters. *The Book of the Dead* describes these waters as existing "in the infinity, the nothingness, the nowhere and the dark."⁶ The *Coffin Texts* describe them as the place where the "Universal Lord dwelt when he was in the infinity, the nothingness and the listlessness." It was a time when "the waters spoke to Infinity, Nothingness, Nowhere, and Darkness."⁷

"Water is formless" comments the translator of these texts, Rundall Clarke. "It has no positive features and of itself assumes no shape. The primeval waters being infinite, all dimensions, directions or spatial qualities of any kind are irrelevant. Nevertheless, the waters are not nothing. They are the basic matter of the universe."⁸

The "Universal Lord" spoken of above, the creator of the Egyptian world stage was, according to the *Coffin Texts,* Atum. "I am ʼAtum," he is represented as saying. "I am he who gave birth to Shu, I am that great He-She, I am he who did what seemed good to him. I took my space in the place of my will. . . ."⁹ Sky was separated from sea, and the top of the primeval mound, the earth world, pushed itself up through the waters into the space between the sea surface and the sky. This is where, according to the Egyptians, the drama of man and creation unfolds. They gave a very striking representation of their world bubble in the image of the celestial goddess Shu crouching on her hands and knees over the outstretched form of the earth-god Geb.

In the *Book of the Dead* Atum warns Osiris that this creation is not permanent.

> Atum: You shall live more than millions of years,
> an era of millions,
> But in the end I will destroy everything
> that I have created

The earth will become again part of the
    Primeval Ocean,
Like the abyss of the waters in their
    original state. . . .
I will have changed myself back into the
    old Serpent
Who knew no man and saw no God.[10]

In another myth, Polynesian this time, it is the created beings themselves which force the separation of the World parents, Rangi and Papa:

> Rangi and Papa, the heaven and the earth, were regarded as the source from which all things, gods and men originated. There was darkness, for these two still clung together, not yet having been rent apart; and the children begotten by them were thinking what the difference between light and darkness might be. They knew that beings had multiplied and increased, and yet light had never broken upon them, but ever darkness. The beings begotten by Rangi and Papa consulted among themselves, saying: "Let us determine what we shall do with Rangi and Papa, whether it be better to slay them or rend them apart."

It was decided to separate the two parents in order to make a space where created beings could live in light and air. Many tried to do so but failed. Finally, the turn of Tanemahatu, the God of forests, birds and insects, came round. At first he too was unsuccessful. But finally "he planted his head on his mother Papa, the earth, and his feet he raised up against Rangi, the sky; he strained his back and his limbs in a mighty effort. Now were rent apart Rangi and Papa, and with reproaches and groans of woe they cried aloud, " 'Why do you thus slay your parents? Why commit so dark a crime as to slay us, to rend your parents, apart?' But Tanemahatu paused not. . . . Far, far beneath him he pressed down Papa the earth; far, far above him he thrust up Rangi, the sky. Hence the saying of old time: 'It was the fiercest thrusting of Tane which tore heaven from earth so that they were rent apart and darkness was made manifest and light made manifest also.' "[11]

Gods and heroes may have different names and the physical setting of myth may vary with time and place, but the symbolical content is constant: only with the separation of opposites, of the fracturing of the primal unity, does the finite world stage come into existence. The symbols are not invented but are "spontaneous productions of the psyche" which bear within themselves the "germ power" of their source.[12]

In its psychic root and in the "germ power" which it conveys all great art partakes of myth. "Both myths and art works," says Wayne Shumaker in *Literature and the Irrational,* "embody states of mind which seek objectified expression because they are affectively charged. . . . The materials within the object are those which, by the modes of their sensory qualities, their affective implications . . . resonate the state of mind which demanded externalization. Observers can then, by allowing the work to *initiate* psychic processes in them, relive the creative experience at a somewhat greater psychological distance."[13] Such art does not so much communicate ideas to the reader as call up within him experiences through which he affectively grasps something of the truth of what it means to be alive and self-conscious in a finite and contingent universe.

IV

The structure of *Un coup de dés* is clear. In his preface Mallarmé says that the whole poem is built around one "motif prépondérant" and another "secondaire." Around these two, he says, are grouped other "adjacent" themes. The primary motif is the central declaration that *Un coup de dés jamais n'abolira le hasard.* The secondary motif—and here I follow the syntactical reconstruction of Gardner Davies—is the conditional statement *si c'était le nombre ce serait le hasard.* In the text these two propositions work out so that they join one another with the word *hasard,* which is at the same time the direct object of *n'abolira* and the predicated noun after *serait.* Schematically it looks like this:

Un coup de dés jamais n'abolira
                    le hasard.
    Si c'était le nombre, ce serait

Of the secondary themes the first, modifying the words "un coup de dés" and introducing the image of a ship on a stormy sea, is that of the first full page: ". . . quand bien même lancé dans des circonstances éternelles, du fond d'un naufrage." The "quand bien même" of this phrase has the function of introducing in a purely hypothetical way the "maître" and the subsequent action involving him. The next minor theme is that of the ninth and tenth pages, which reflects on the consequences of this action, should it in reality occur: ". . . rien n'aura eu lieu que le lieu, excepté peut-être une constellation." Finally, appended as a coda to the entire account is the bare, simple statement: "Toute pensée émet un coup de dés."

Paul Valéry has told of the day and evening at Valvins when Mallarmé first showed him his manuscript of *Un coup de dés*. "Il me sembla voir," recounts Valéry,

> La figure d'une pensée, pour la première fois placée dans notre espace. . . . L'Attente, le doute, la concentration étaient *choses visibles*. Ma vue avait affaire à des silences qui aurait pris corps. Je contemplais à mon aise d'inappréciables instants: la fraction d'une seconde pendant laquelle s'étonne, brille, s'anéantit une idée; l'atome de temps, germes de siècles psychologiques et de conséquences infinies, —paraissaient comme des êtres, tout environnés de leur néant rendu sensible. C'était . . . toute une tempête spirituelle menée de page en page, jusqu'à un point d'ineffable rupture. . . .

Later in the evening as the two men walked through the summer night to the station where Valéry was to board a train for Paris, the younger man suddenly grasped the infinite intent of the poem:

> Le soir du même jour, comme il m'accompagnait au chemin de fer, l'innombrable ciel de juillet enfermant toutes choses dans un groupe étincelant d'autres mondes et que nous marchions, fumeurs obscurs, au milieu du Serpent, du Cygne, de l'Aigle, de la Lyre, —il me semblait *maintenant* d'être pris dans le texte

même de l'univers silencieux: texte tout de clartés et d'énigmes: aussi tragique, aussi indifférent qu'on le veut: qui parle et qui ne parle pas; tissu de sens multiples; qui assemble l'ordre et le désordre; qui proclame un Dieu aussi puissamment qu'il le nie; qui contient, dans son ensemble inimaginable, toutes les époques, chacune associée à l'éloignement d'un corps céleste: qui rappelle le plus décisif, le plus évident et incontestable succès des hommes, l'accomplissement de leurs prévisions,— jusqu'à la septième décimale; et qui écrase cet animal témoin, ce contemplateur sagace, sous l'inutilité de ce triomphe . . . Nous marchions. Au creux d'une telle nuit, entre les propos que nous échangions, je songeais à la tentative merveilleuse: quel modèle, quel enseignement, là-haut! Où Kant, assez naïvement, peut-être, avait cru voir la Loi Morale, Mallarmé percevait sans doute l'Impératif d'une poésie: une Poétique.

Cette dispersion radieuse: ces buissons pales et ardents: ces semences presque spirituelles, distinctes et simultanés; l'immense interrogation qui se propose par ce silence chargé de tant de vie et de tant de mort, tout cela, gloire par soi-même, total étrange de réalité et d'idéaux contradictoires, ne devait-il pas suggérer à quelqu'un la suprême tentation d'en reproduire l'effet!

"Il a essayé," pensai-je, *"d'enlever enfin une page à la puissance du ciel étoilé!"*[14]

The universality of the "circonstances éternelles" of the poem, the birth, brilliance, and death of idea and star, the momentary triumph of consciousness and a sense of the "uselessness" of that triumph with respect to its absolute ambitions, —Valéry, participating in a mythic recapitulation of an archetypal happening, grasped all of these themes immediately and almost without reflection.

For if "Un coup de dés" is obscure with regard to grammar and syntax, it is very clear as myth. The adventure takes place on the surface of the primeval ocean. The clouds are low, there is very little space, and what there is seems in danger of disappearing. The force which has separated the opposites, the "réciproques néants" of heaven and sea, cannot forever be maintained. Within that space, the "maître" has freed himself from the unconscious womb of the waters and has surged up into view, at least for the time required for the accomplishment of his "geste." Will he act? He hesitates. He knows that no spatial and temporal act can wholly escape the limitations of the conditions which make it possible. He makes the gesture and falls immediately back into the waters. Behind him remains only a dull flat lapping of the waters, "un inférieur clapotis quelconque." No evidence remains of his struggle except, perhaps, "aussi loin qu'un endroit fusionne avec l'au-delà" a constellation against the black sky. But even the constellation, for all its cold remoteness and purity, lies short of its goal. The "septentrion aussi Nord," the Great Bear, eternally circles the polar star, the primal point and unitary source of all creation, as though in rapt adoration but without diminishing at all the distance which separates it from the goal toward which it longs.[15]

Not even the poet-mystic can reproduce his "eternal" reminiscences in a physical work of art, for every work of man is hopelessly contaminated by time. No matter how perfect the poem, no matter how clearly it points the way, it can never coincide with its object, just as the constellation is never swallowed up again into the polar star. Igitur knew it and Hérodiade knew it. The work of art—or any other spiritual work—remains, even in its greatness, a vain and doomed attempt to restore edenic wholeness while yet retaining the life of consciousness. "There is no rest short of complete fulfillment of being," wrote Meister Eckhart. But such fulfillment is not possible short of death.

Notes

1. Blakney, *Eckhart*, pp. 192–193.
2. Valéry, *Œuvres*, p. 625.
3. *The Origins and History of Consciousness* (New York, 1954), p. 12.
4. *Ibid.*, p. 4.
5. *Ibid.*, p. 47.
6. Rundall Clarke, *Myth and Symbol in Ancient Egypt* (London, 1959), p. 56.
7. *Ibid.*, p. 57.

8. *Ibid.*, p. 36.

9. *Ibid.*, p. 14.

10. *Ibid.*, p. 175.

11. Quoted by Neumann from Anderson, *Myths and Legends of the Polynesians*, pp. 367–368.

12. Joseph Campbell, *The Myth of the Hero* (New York, 1949), p. 4.

13. New York, 1960, pp. 153–154.

14. Valéry, *Œuvres*, I, 624–625.

15. I have found support for some of the details of my reading of *Un coup de dés*, particularly in its cosmogonic aspect, as well as for my reading of *Sainte* and other poems in R. G. Cohn's fine book, *Toward the Poems of Mallarmé* (Los Angeles, 1965).

Bibliography

Abrams, M. H. *The Mirror and the Lamp: Romantic Theory and the Critical Tradition.* New York: Norton, 1958.

Aish, D. A. K. *La métaphore dans l'œuvre de Stéphane Mallarmé.* Paris: Droz, 1938.

Ayda, Adile. *Le drame intérieur de Mallarmé.* Istanbul: La Turquie Moderne, 1955.

Bird, Edward A. *L'univers poétique de Stéphane Mallarmé.* Paris: Nizet, 1962.

Blakney, Raymond B. *Meister Eckhart.* New York: Harper, 1941.

Bowra, C. M. *The Heritage of Symbolism.* London: Macmillan, 1943.

Brémond, Henri. *La poésie pure.* Paris: Grasset, 1926.

Broad, C. D. *Religion, Philosophy, and Psychical Research.* New York: Harcourt, Brace, 1953.

Bucke, R. M. *The Cosmic Consciousness.* Philadelphia: E. P. Dutton, 1901.

Campbell, Joseph. *The Myth of the Hero.* New York: Pantheon, 1949.

Castex, Pierre-Georges, ed. *Autour du symbolisme.* Paris: Jose Corti, 1955.

Chassé, Charles. *Lueurs sur Mallarmé.* Paris: Nouvelle Revue critique, 1947.

Chisholm, A. R. *Towards Hérodiade.* Melbourne: Melbourne University Press, 1934.

Cirlot, J. E. *A Dictionary of Symbols.* New York: Philosophical Library, 1962.

Clarke, Rundall. *Myth and Symbol in Ancient Egypt.* London: Thames and Hudson, 1959.

Cohn, R. G. *Mallarmé's Un coup de dés.* New Haven: Yale University Press, 1949.

Cohn, R. G. *Mallarmé's Masterwork: New Findings.* The Hague: Mouton, 1966.

———. *Toward the Poems of Mallarmé.* Los Angeles: University of California Press, 1965.

Cornell, Kenneth. *The Symbolist Movement.* New Haven: Yale University Press, 1951.

Crane, Hart. *The Collected Poems of Hart Crane.* New York: Liveright, 1946.

――――. *The Letters of Hart Crane, 1916–1932,* ed. Brom Weber. Berkeley: University of California Press, 1952.

Davies, Gardner. *Vers une explication rationelle du Coup de dés.* Paris: Jose Corti, 1953.

Delfel, Guy. *L'esthétique de Stéphane Mallarmé.* Paris: Flammarion, 1951.

――――. *Mallarmé, pages choisies.* Paris: Hachette, 1954.

Ellmann, Richard. *W. B. Yeats: The Man and the Masks.* New York: E. P. Dutton, 1958.

Ewer, Mary Anita. *A Survey of Mystical Symbolism.* London: S.P.C.K., 1933.

Faulkner, William. *Light in August.* New York: Modern Library, 1950.

Festugière, A. J. *La révélation d'Hermès Trismégiste.* Paris: Lecoffre, 1950.

Fowlie, Wallace. *Mallarmé.* Chicago: University of Chicago Press, 1953.

――――. *Mallarmé as Hamlet: A Study of Igitur.* New York: The Atheist Bookshop Press, 1949.

Frazer, Sir James George. *The New Golden Bough.* New York: Criterion, 1961.

Frétet, Jean. *L'aliénation poétique.* Paris: Janin, 1946.

Gengoux, Jacques. *Le symbolisme de Mallarmé.* Paris: Nizet, 1950.

Guthrie, W. C. K. *Orpheus and Greek Religion.* London: Methuen, 1952.

Holmyard, E. J. *Alchemy.* London: Penguin Books, 1957.

Huxley, Aldous. *The Doors of Perception.* London: Chatto & Windus, 1954.

James, William. *The Varieties of Religious Experience.* New York: Random House, 1946.

St. John of the Cross. *The Dark Night of the Soul,* trans. and ed. Kurt F. Reinhardt. New York: Frederick Ungar, 1957.

Joyce, James. *The Portrait of the Artist as a Young Man.* New York: The Viking Press, 1964.

Jung, C. G. *Archetypes of the Collective Unconscious.* New York: Pantheon, 1959.

Koestler, Arthur. *The Invisible Writing.* New York: Macmillan, 1954.

Leuba, James H. *The Psychology of Religious Mysticism.* New York: Harcourt, Brace, 1925.

Macchioro, Vittorio D. *From Orpheus to Paul.* New York: Henry Holt, 1930.

Macintyre, C. F. *French Symbolist Poetry*. Berkeley: University of California Press, 1954.

Mallarmé, Stéphane. *Œuvres complètes,* ed. Henri Mondor and Jean Aubry. Paris: Gallimard, 1945.

————. *Correspondance I 1862–1871,* ed. Mondor and Richard. Paris: Gallimard, 1959.

————. *Correspondance, II. 1871–1885,* ed. Mondor and Austin. Paris: Gallimard, 1965.

————. *Divagations*. Paris: Fasquelle, 1897.

————. *Propos sur la poésie,* ed. Henri Mondor. Monaco: Editions du Rocher, 1946.

————. *Un coup de dés*. Paris: N. R. F., 1914.

Maritain, Jacques. *Art et scholastique*. Paris: Louise Rouart et Fils, 1927.

————. *Creative Intuition in Art and Poetry*. New York: World, 1953.

Mauron, Charles. *Introduction à la psychanalyse de Mallarmé*. Neuchâtel: La Baconnière, 1950.

————. *Mallarmé l'obscur*. Paris: Denoël, 1941.

May, Rollo, ed. *Symbolism in Religion and Literature*. New York: Braziller, 1961.

Michaud, Guy. *Mallarmé, l'homme et l'œuvre*. Paris: Hatier-Boivin, 1953.

————. *Message poétique du symbolisme*. 3 vols. Paris: Nizet, 1947.

Mondor, Henri. *Histoire d'un faune*. Paris: Gallimard, 1948.

————. *Mallarmé plus intime*. Paris: Gallimard, 1944.

————. *Vie de Mallarmé*. Paris: Gallimard, 1942.

Neumann, Erich. *The Origins and History of Consciousness*. New York: Harper Torchbooks, 1954.

Noulet, Emilie. *L'oeuvre poétique de Stéphane Mallarmé*. Paris: Droz, 1948.

————. *Dix poèmes de Stéphane Mallarmé*. Lille: Giard, 1948.

Perse, St.-Jean. *On Poetry*. Bollingen, 1961.

Raymond, Marcel. *De Baudelaire au surréalisme*. Paris: Correa, 1933.

Richard, Jean-Pierre. *L'univers imaginaire de Mallarmé*. Paris: Editions du Seuil, 1961.

Rimbaud, Arthur. *Œuvres complètes*. Paris: Gallimard, 1954.

Saurat, Denis. *Literature and the Occult Tradition*. London: G. Bell and Sons, 1930.

Scott, Walter. *Hermetica*. Oxford: Clarendon Press, 1924.

Schérer, Jacques, ed. *Le livre de Mallarmé*. Paris: Gallimard, 1957.

Scholem, G. G. *La kabbale et sa symbolique*. Paris: Payot, 1966.

Senior, John. *The Way Down and Out: The Occult in Symbolist Literature*. Ithaca: Cornell University Press, 1959.

Seward, Barbara. *The Symbolic Rose*. New York: Columbia University Press, 1960.

Shumaker, Wayne. *Literature and the Irrational*. Englewood Cliffs: Prentice Hall, 1960.

Simon, Maurice, trans. *Zohar,* 5 vols. Bennett Publications, n. p., n. d.

Soula, Camille. *Gloses sur Mallarmé*. Paris: Diderot, 1946.

———. *La poésie et la pensée de Stéphane Mallarmé*. Paris: Champion, 1926.

———. *Un coup de dés*. Paris: Champion, 1931.

Stace, W. T. *Mysticism and Philosophy*. Philadelphia: Lippincott, 1960.

Stiernotte, Alfred P., ed. *Mysticism and the Modern Mind*. New York: Liberal Arts Press, 1959.

Suzuki, D. T. *Mysticism: Christian and Buddhist*. New York: Harper, 1957.

Symons, Arthur. *The Symbolist Movement in Literature*. New York: E. P. Dutton, 1958.

Thibaudet, Albert. *La poésie de Stéphane Mallarmé*. Paris: Gallimard, 1926.

Tindall, William York. *The Literary Symbol*. New York: Columbia University Press, 1955.

Trobridge, George. *Swedenborg, Life and Teaching*. New York: Swedenborg Foundation, 1938.

The Upanishads, trans. Swami Prabhavanada and Frederick Manchester. New York: New American Library, 1957.

Underhill, Evelyn. *The Essentials of Mysticism and Other Essays*. New York: E. P. Dutton, 1960.

———. *Mysticism*. New York: E. P. Dutton, 1961.

Valéry, Paul. *Œuvres*. 2 vols. Paris: Gallimard, 1958.

Viatte, Auguste. *Les sources occultes du romantisme*. Paris: Champion, 1928.

Waite, A. E. *The Holy Kabbalah*. New York: University Books, n. d.

Wheelwright, Philip. *The Burning Fountain*. Bloomington: Indiana University Press, 1954.

Yates, F. A. *Giordano Bruno and the Hermetic Tradition*. Chicago: University of Chicago Press, 1964.

Yeats, W. B. *The Autobiography of William Butler Yeats*. Garden City: Doubleday, 1958.

Zimmer, Heinrich. *Myths and Symbols in Indian Art and Civilization*. New York: Pantheon, 1946.

Index

DATE DUE